A Midsummer Night's Dream

HEINEMANN

SHAKESPEARE

A Midsummer Night's Dream

edited by Elizabeth Seely

with additional material by
Cherry Stephenson,
John Seely,
Rick Lee

Series Editor: John Seely

*In association with the RSA
Shakespeare in Schools Project*

The RSA Shakespeare in Schools Project

The **Heinemann Shakespeare Series** has been developed in association with the **RSA Shakespeare in Schools Project**. Schools in the project have trialled teaching approaches to make Shakespeare accessible to students of all ages and ability levels.

John Seely has worked with schools in the project to develop the unique way of teaching Shakespeare to 11 to 16-year-olds found in **Heinemann Shakespeares**.

The project is a partnership between the RSA (Royal Society for the encouragement of Arts, Manufactures and Commerce), Leicestershire County Council and the Groby family of schools in Leicestershire. It is co-ordinated by the Knighton Fields Advisory Centre for Drama and Dance.

We would particularly like to acknowledge South Charnwood School for the contribution to *A Midsummer Night's Dream*.

Heinemann Educational Publishers
Halley Court, Jordan Hill, Oxford OX2 8EJ
Part of Harcourt Education

Heinemann is the registered trademark of Harcourt Educational Limited

The text is taken from the Players' Shakespeare edition

Published in the *Heinemann Shakespeare* series 1993

12

A catalogue record for this book is available from the British Library on request.
ISBN 0 435 19202 7

Cover design Miller Craig and Cocking
Cover photograph from Donald Cooper

Typeset by Taurus Graphics, Kidlington, Oxon

Printed in the UK by Clays Ltd, St Ives plc

Contents

Introduction: using this book

This is more than just an edition of *A Midsummer Night's Dream* with a few notes. It is a complete guide to studying and enjoying the play.

It begins with an introduction to Shakespeare's theatre, and to the story and characters of the play.

At the end of the book there is guidance on studying the play:
- how to keep track of things as you work
- how to take part in a range of drama activities
- understanding Shakespeare's language
- exploring the main themes of love and friendship: dreams and magic
- studying the characters
- how to write about the play.

There are also practice questions and a glossary of specialist words you need when working on the play.

The central part of the book is, of course, the play itself. Here there are several different kinds of help on offer:

Summary: at the top of each page there is a short summary of what happens on that page.

Grading: alongside the text is a shaded band to help you when working on the play:

1 This is very important text that you probably need to spend extra time on.
2 This is text that you need to read carefully.
3 This is text that you need to spend less time on.

Notes: difficult words, phrases and sentences are explained in simple English

Extra summaries: for the 'white' text the notes are replaced by numbered summaries that give more detail than the ordinary page-by-page summaries.

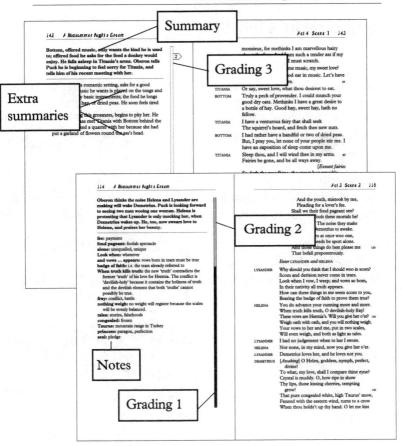

Summary

Extra summaries

Grading 3

Grading 2

Notes

Grading 1

Activities

Every few scenes there is a section containing things to do,
helping you focus on the scenes you have just read:

- questions to make sure you have understood the story
- discussion points about the themes and characters of the
  play
- drama activities
- character work
- close study to help you focus on a section of the text in
  more detail
- writing activities

Shakespeare's theatre

Heavens (A)
the roof above the stage,
supported by pillars. Characters
could be lowered to the stage
during the play

Gallery (B)
used for action on an upper level
(or, if not, for the musicians)

Inner space (C)
curtained area that could be
opened up to show a new scene

*Standing space for
audience*

Doors (D)
used by the actors, leading from
the stage to the tiring house
(dressing rooms)

Stage (E)
the acting area was very
big and had trapdoors
so that actors could enter
from underneath the
stage floor.

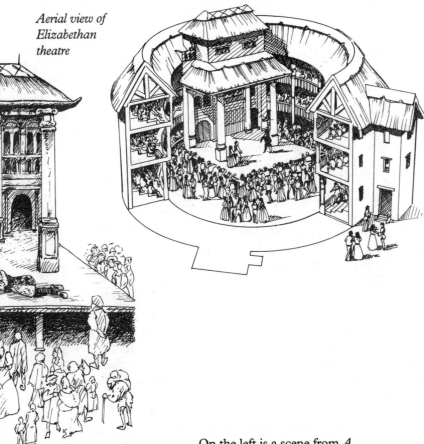

Aerial view of Elizabethan theatre

On the left is a scene from *A Midsummer Night's Dream* showing both the inner stage and the gallery in use for the action of the play.

When you have studied the play you should be able to work out exactly which moment in the play this shows.

Going to the theatre in Shakespeare's day

Theatre going was very popular in Elizabethan London, but it was very different from going to a play today. It was like a cross between going to a football match and going to the theatre. The playhouses were open air and the lack of artificial lighting meant that plays were performed in daylight, normally in the afternoon.

Places were not reserved, so people had to arrive in plenty of time - often more than an hour before the play was due to start. They paid a penny to get into the playhouse, so it was not cheap, since a penny was about one twelfth of a day's wages for a skilled workman. Your penny let you into the large open yard surrounding the stage. The audience here had to stand, looking up at the actors (the stage was 1.5-1.8 metres high). If people wanted a seat, then they had to pay another penny or twopence. This gave admission to the tiers of seating surrounding the yard, and also meant that you had a roof over your head, in case it started to rain. People with even more money could pay to have a seat in an enclosed room. So people of all incomes and social classes attended the theatre and paid for the kind of accommodation they wanted.

While the audience were waiting for the play to begin they had time to meet friends, talk, eat and drink - in fact people used to continue to enjoy themselves in this way while the play was being performed. But Elizabethan audiences were knowledgeable and enthusiastic. Watching a play was an exciting experience; although the stage was very big, the theatre was quite small, so no one was far from the actors. When an actor had a soliloquy (solo speech) he could come right into the middle of the audience and speak his thoughts in a natural, personal way. At the other extreme the large stage and the three different levels meant that whole battles could be enacted, complete with cannon fire, thunder and lightning and loud military music.

There was no painted stage scenery, so that the audience had to use their imagination to picture the location of each scene, but Shakespeare always gave plenty of word clues in the characters' speeches of when and where a scene takes place. The lack of scenery to move about also meant that scene could follow scene without any break. On the other hand, the theatre companies spared no expense on costumes and furniture and other properties; plays also had live music performed by players placed either in the auditorium close to the stage, or in the gallery above it, if that was not to be used in the play.

Altogether Londoners especially must have considered that going to the theatre was an exciting and important part of their lives; it is believed that up to a fifth of them went to the theatre regularly. Shakespeare and the company in which he became a shareholder, the Lord Chamberlain's Men, worked hard and became wealthy men.

The story of the play

Act 1

Scene 1

Theseus, Duke of Athens and **Hippolyta** are looking forward to their wedding in four days' time.

Their happy mood is interrupted by the arrival of **Egeus** and his daughter **Hermia**, and two young men, **Lysander** and **Demetrius**, both of whom want to marry her. Egeus complains to the Duke, that his daughter is refusing to marry Demetrius, her father's choice. Egeus demands the death penalty for her disobedience.

Hermia is in love with Lysander. She insists, even to the Duke, that she will not marry Demetrius. Lysander points out that Demetrius had previously been in love with another young woman called **Helena**, but he has changed his mind.

Theseus tells Hermia that she must either obey her father and marry Demetrius or be put to death. He cannot make her change her decision, but tells her the penalty is either death or life in a convent. He warns her that she will not be happy as a nun, and gives her the four days until his own wedding to make her choice.

Hermia and Lysander agree that they will meet in the wood the following evening and will go to Lysander's aunt's house, where, away from the power of Athenian law, they can safely be married. They tell Helena, who is Hermia's childhood friend, of their plan. She is still desperately in love with Demetrius and decides to betray them to him and then go to the wood herself, so that she can at least be near him.

Scene 2

Six Athenian workmen have been chosen to put on a play

for the royal wedding celebrations. They hold a meeting to cast their play, which is a tragedy about the forbidden love and the death of the lovers Pyramus and Thisby. Although **Peter Quince**, a carpenter, is in charge and has cast the play, **Bottom**, a weaver, keeps interrupting and is full of ideas about every part that is mentioned. They arrange to meet in the wood for their rehearsal, so that their plans will remain a secret.

Act 2

Scene 1

Puck, who is the servant of **Oberon**, the Fairy King, meets a fairy who serves **Titania**, the Fairy Queen. Puck explains that the fairy kingdom has been split by a serious quarrel between Oberon and Titania over the ownership of an Indian child. Oberon wants the boy to be one of his pages and Titania refuses to give him up. The fairy recognises Puck as the sprite who is famous for playing practical jokes on humans. He can make himself invisible or take on different shapes.

Oberon and Titania meet, still quarrelling. Titania claims that as a result of their dispute, the weather and the seasons are all at odds and humans are suffering. She explains why she wants to keep the child.

Oberon decides to punish Titania and force her to part with the boy. He uses Puck to fetch a magic flower. When the juice of this plant is squeezed on sleeping eyelids, the man or woman treated with it will fall madly in love with the first creature seen on awaking.

Oberon watches Helena and Demetrius together. She is still chasing Demetrius and will not leave him alone although he speaks very cruelly to her. Oberon tells Puck to treat Demetrius with the juice so that he will fall in love with Helena.

Scene 2

Titania's fairies lull her to sleep and set a guard, but because Oberon is invisible he is able to squeeze the magic juice on Titania's eyelids.

Hermia and Lysander have lost their way in the wood and decide to sleep till morning. Because they are not yet married, Hermia will not let Lysander sleep very close to her.

While they are asleep Puck mistakenly applies the juice to Lysander's eyes, thinking he is Demetrius.

Helena can no longer keep up with Demetrius. Left behind, she sees Lysander lying on the ground and thinking he may be wounded or dead, wakes him up. The result of Puck's mistake is that Lysander now falls madly in love with Helena, who thinks it is all a pretence and done to make fun of her. Lysander leaves Hermia asleep on the ground, saying he hates her now, and follows Helena. Hermia then wakes up from a nightmare in which a snake was eating her heart, while Lysander looked on, smiling. She is very anxious and hurt that Lysander has left her without a word.

Act 3

Scene 1

Without realising it, of course, since Titania is invisible, the workmen are rehearsing near where she is sleeping. Puck chances on the workmen's rehearsal. This gives him an idea to help Oberon in his plans and he puts an ass's head on Bottom who is waiting for his cue. When Bottom's friends see it they run off in terror and Puck leads them around the wood, taking on different shapes. Bottom sings to show he is not afraid. This wakes Titania up and she falls in love with him. She gives him fairies to wait on him, and they go away together.

Scene 2

Puck tells Oberon what has happened to Titania and he is very pleased. He is not so pleased, however, when he realises that Puck has put the juice on the wrong lover's eyes.

Hermia, abandoned by Lysander, has gone off in search of him but finds Demetrius, who is still in love with her. He is looking for Lysander so that he can kill him.

Hermia accuses Demetrius of having already killed Lysander. He denies it. They quarrel and, when she runs off, Demetrius falls asleep. Oberon sends Puck to bring Helena along and puts the juice on Demetrius' eyes at last.

Lysander is desperately trying to prove to Helena how much he loves her. He is in tears. She insists that Hermia is the one he loves and is sure it is all a cruel joke. Helena and Lysander argue so loudly that they wake Demetrius. The first person he sees is Helena and he declares his love for her.

When Hermia comes looking for Lysander, she too is bewildered, but Helena thinks they are all in a plot to make a fool of her. Soon there is a four-sided quarrel going on. It becomes so serious that Hermia tries to claw Helena's face with her nails, and Lysander and Demetrius go off to fight a duel over Helena. The two women, angry and hurt, go off in different directions.

Oberon will not allow a duel to result from Puck's mistake and sends him to mislead the two men. He keeps them apart till they lie down to sleep from exhaustion. Soon Hermia and Helena separately find the same spot in the dark and they too fall asleep. Puck treats Lysander's eyes with the juice of another plant. This is the antidote to the love-juice.

Oberon watches the results of his revenge on Titania while she sleeps with Bottom asleep in her arms. He had remonstrated with her earlier about her infatuation with Bottom and she gave up the child to him. He removes the magic with the antidote and they are happy together again. Puck is instructed to remove the ass's head from Bottom, and to lay a deep sleep over him and the four lovers.

Act 4

Scene 1

Theseus and Hippolyta, with some of their courtiers, including Egeus, are out early in the forest to celebrate Midsummer Day and to go hunting. Theseus proudly shows off his hounds to his fiancée, who knows a lot about the subject. They stumble on the four lovers, and wake them up.

Egeus is furious when he learns that Lysander and Hermia had planned to elope, but Demetrius declares his love for Helena. So Theseus, realising that the couples are now happily paired, decides that this is the right outcome. He announces that all three couples shall be married at a triple wedding ceremony. Still bewildered, they all follow the Duke. Bottom, with ass's head removed, wakes up, still under the influence of his amazing experience. He feels it was a 'most rare vision' and wants Quince to write a ballad about it.

The other workmen are very concerned at Bottom's disappearance, because without him their play cannot be put on. They also think the Duke might have rewarded them for their performance. Bottom arrives back just in time for the play to go ahead. He promises to tell them his story later and tells them to get ready for the play.

Act 5

Scene 1

Theseus and Hippolyta are discussing the lovers' story. Theseus puts it down to tricks of the imagination but Hippolyta is more inclined to think that something odd really did happen.

Theseus greets the lovers and considers which of the many possible entertainments to have that evening. Philostrate has seen the workmen's play in rehearsal and advises against it, but Theseus overrules him since it has been prepared with love and duty.

The workmen present their play with the court and the lovers commenting on it - Bottom in the role of Pyramus returns from the dead to comment on their comments. They follow their play with a dance. It is after midnight and Theseus suggests it is time for bed. There will be two weeks of celebrations.

Puck prepares the way for Oberon and Titania. The Fairy King and Queen and all their followers dance through the house bringing blessings to all the newly-weds, and any children they may have.

Puck brings the play to an end, apologising for any offence given and claiming that all the action can be regarded as a dream.

Separate strands

It is quite easy to get confused by the story of *A Midsummer Night's Dream*. This is partly because it is not really one story, but four. On the next pages, these four stories are told separately.

Theseus and Hippolyta

Act 1 scene 1

Theseus, Duke of Athens, and Hippolyta, Queen of the Amazons, are looking forward to their wedding in four days' time. Great celebrations are planned.

Egeus brings a complaint against his daughter, Hermia. He has chosen Demetrius as a husband for her but she is in love with someone else – Lysander. Egeus is demanding her obedience or her death.

Theseus tells Hermia she should obey her father. By law she must choose between obedience, death or life as a nun. She must give her choice on Theseus' wedding day.

When Theseus is reminded that Demetrius has previously been in love with a girl called Helena, who still worships him, he takes Demetrius and Egeus off for a private conversation.

Act 4 scene 1

Early on Midsummer morning Theseus and Hippolyta are out in the woods. They intend to hunt, but suddenly they stumble across the four lovers, fast asleep. Egeus is furious that Lysander and Hermia had meant to run away, but Theseus, realising that all four are now happily paired, overrules Egeus and suggests a joint wedding ceremony.

Act 5 scene 1

Hippolyta and Theseus, now married, discuss the lovers' stories about the previous night. He thinks it is all imagination, she believes them.

Intrigued by the contradictions it offers, Theseus chooses the workmen's play 'Pyramus and Thisby' for the evening's entertainment. He assures Hippolyta that he has learnt to understand people's intentions, rather than their success or failure.

They both comment on the play, wittily but not cruelly. It is after midnight when Theseus thanks the players and brings the evening to a close, promising a fortnight of celebrations.

Lysander and Hermia, Demetrius and Helena

Act 1 scene 1
Hermia is brought to the court by her father, Egeus, because she refuses to marry her father's choice for her, Demetrius. She is deeply in love with Lysander, whom Egeus will not accept. Egeus insists on her obedience or her death.

Theseus confirms that the law demands her obedience, her death or life as a nun.

Lysander and Demetrius state their claim. Lysander says Demetrius has previously been in love with Helena, who still worships him. Hermia is left to make her decision within the next four days.

Lysander and Hermia agree to run away together to his aunt's house, and marry where Athenian law cannot reach them. They will meet the following night in the wood. Helena is very unhappy that Demetrius no longer loves her and is both jealous and envious of Hermia. Lysander and Hermia tell Helena of their plans, but she then decides to betray them to Demetrius and follow him to the wood.

Act 2 scene 1
Helena chases Demetrius through the wood. He speaks cruelly to her and goes off to find and kill Lysander, still followed by Helena.

Oberon, the Fairy King, has been watching this, takes pity on Helena and tells Puck to treat Demetrius' eyes with magic love-juice.

Act 2 scene 2

Lysander and Hermia lose their way in the wood and decide to sleep until daylight. Hermia will not let Lysander lie too close.

Puck, who is actually looking for Demetrius, finds Lysander and doses his eyes with magic juice by mistake. The juice will make Lysander fall desperately in love with the first creature he sees when he wakes up.

Helena can no longer keep up with Demetrius. She sees Lysander lying on the ground and wakes him up. He instantly falls in love with her. She believes he is mocking her and goes. Before Lysander follows her, he stands over the still-sleeping Hermia saying how much he hates her. Hermia wakes up from a nightmare. She is alarmed that Lysander has disappeared and goes off to find him.

Act 3 scene 2

Hermia comes in with Demetrius. She is looking for Lysander and assumes that Demetrius has killed him. She invites him to kill her too. Demetrius says he is innocent. She leaves.

Demetrius is tired out and lies down to sleep. Oberon takes this opportunity to put the magic juice on his eyes. Meanwhile Lysander, in tears, is trying to convince Helena of his love. She will not believe it because she knows he loves Hermia. While they are arguing Demetrius wakes up and falls in love with Helena. She thinks they've teamed up to make fun of her. Hermia now joins them, delighted at finding Lysander. She is shocked and hurt when he says he hates her now. Helena thinks she is part of the conspiracy to mock her.

Now both Lysander and Demetrius are rivals for Helena's love. They decide to fight a duel. The women turn on each other and nearly fight but Helena runs away and Hermia leaves.

Puck leads the men apart in a magic fog. First Lysander lies down, exhausted, and falls asleep, then Demetrius. Helena, worn out, lies down too, and finally Hermia. All are in the same clearing, but all unseen by the others.

Act 4 scene 1

When the huntsman wakes them, Lysander tries to explain matters to the Duke. Egeus wants Lysander punished, but Demetrius now declares that Helena is his only true love for ever. The Duke tells Egeus the lovers should stay happily paired, as they are. They follow the Duke back to Athens and are married.

Titania, Oberon and Puck

Act 2 scene 1

Puck, Oberon's servant, meets one of Titania's fairies. Puck is famous for playing tricks on humans, but can bring good luck too.

Titania and Oberon have quarrelled over the possession of an Indian child. Oberon wants Titania to give him the boy as one of his attendants. She refuses. Oberon and Titania meet. They have come because of the royal wedding and they accuse one another of having loved Hippolyta and Theseus. Titania claims that all the seasons have been at odds since their squabble. She refuses to part with the boy and explains why. They part, still very angry.

Oberon plans to blackmail her into parting with the child. He tells Puck to fetch a magic flower, the juice of which, laid on sleeping eyes, will make the victim fall hopelessly in love with the first live creature seen. There is an antidote which can remove the charm.

While Puck is away, Oberon watches Demetrius being unkind to Helena and decides that Puck shall put some of the magic juice on Demetrius' eyes.

Once Oberon has the juice he finds Titania asleep and applies the juice to her eyes.

Puck mistakes Lysander for Demetrius and so puts the juice on Lysander's eyes.

Act 3 scene 1

Puck watches the workmen's play rehearsal and puts an ass's head on Bottom. Titania falls in love with Bottom. Oberon is delighted when Puck tells him what he has done. When Oberon and Puck watch Hermia and Demetrius they realise that Puck has treated the wrong man. Oberon is angry with Puck and sends him to fetch Helena. Meanwhile Oberon treats the eyelids of the sleeping Demetrius. He and Puck watch as both Demetrius and Lysander declare their love for Helena and she rejects it all as cruel mockery. When Demetrius and Lysander go off, intending to fight a duel, Puck is told to create a magic fog and to keep them apart. When all the lovers have lain down to sleep he squeezes the juice on Lysander's eyes.

Act 4 scene 1

Oberon watches Titania with Bottom. He feels both jealousy and pity. As she has given him the child he will release her from the spell. Puck is to release Bottom also. Oberon wakes Titania, who now loathes the sight of Bottom. A deep sleep is laid over the lovers and Bottom. Friends again, Oberon and Titania dance.

Act 5

Puck comes to prepare the house for the night. Oberon, Titania and the fairies bless the house, the marriages and the future children of all three couples. Puck ends the play with an apology for any offence and the suggestion that perhaps the audience has been dreaming too.

Bottom and the workmen

Act 1 scene 1

Six Athenian workmen meet to discuss putting on a play as part of the royal wedding celebrations. The play is about the forbidden love of Pyramus and Thisby. Quince is the producer and he gives the part of Pyramus to Bottom, the weaver. Having cast the play they agree to meet on the following evening in the wood.

Act 3 scene 1
They meet near where Titania is asleep. To avoid frightening their audience they must explain away the sword and the lion.

They start rehearsing, misreading words and ignoring their cues. Puck comes past and stays to watch. After Bottom's first exit Puck puts an ass's head on him. All Bottom's friends run away in terror and Puck plans to lead them all around the dark wood.

Bottom stays and sings to keep his courage up. Titania hears him and falls in love with him. She gives him fairies to wait on him and takes him away with her.

Act 4 scene 1
Titania is caressing her new love. She offers him music and food. He prefers things he is used to. Soon he falls asleep in her arms.

While Bottom sleeps, Oberon takes the charm off Titania's eyes and Puck removes the ass's head from Bottom. He is still in a magically deep sleep. When he wakes up he remembers the strange things he has seen and feels the need to write about it.

His friends are very concerned about him. Bottom suddenly reappears, promising to tell them his story, but hustling them to get ready for the play.

Act 5
The workmen's play is to be the evening's entertainment. The prologue says the opposite of what Quince means, because he is so nervous. All the characters are introduced and the play goes ahead. The audience is entertained and comments freely. A couple of times Bottom cannot help putting the Duke right. Bottom clearly enjoys the role of Pyramus and his bloody death.

Theseus chooses a dance to end the programme. The players are thanked and leave.

The characters of the play

There are four distinct groups of characters in the play.
Each group has its own strand but the stories are constantly
interwoven until they all come together in the final act
of the play.

Theseus

Hippolyta

Egeus

The Athenian Court
Theseus, the Duke and
his fianceé, **Hippolyta**
and their attendants.
Egeus, Hermia's father,
belongs loosely to this
group as he tries to use
the court's power to
make his daughter
marry Demetrius.

Demetrius

The Lovers
Hermia and **Lysander** and
Helena and **Demetrius**. The
lovers go through various
traumas before ending up
'happy ever after'.

Helena

Hermia Lysander

Puck

heartsease

The Fairies
Oberon, the Fairy King and **Titania**, the Fairy Queen and their followers. Oberon and Titania have a lot of power and their quarrelling has upset the weather and seasons. A lot of the lovers' problems and also the happy ending are due to the external magic caused by Oberon and **Puck**. Puck is Oberon's go-between although he has a lively and entertaining magic career of his own.

Bottom

ass's head

Oberon   *Titania*

The Athenian Workmen
who have been chosen to put on a play to entertain Theseus and Hippolyta at court after their wedding. **Quince** is in charge of the group but **Bottom** has his own ideas about everything.

Quince, Snug, Flute Starveling

A Midsummer Night's Dream

Characters

THESEUS, Duke of Athens
EGEUS, father to Hermia
LYSANDER
DEMETRIUS } in love with Hermia
PHILOSTRATE, Master of the Revels to Theseus
PETER QUINCE, a carpenter
SNUG, a joiner
NICK BOTTOM, a weaver
FRANCIS FLUTE, a bellows-mender
TOM SNOUT, a tinker
ROBIN STARVELING, a tailor
HIPPOLYTA, Queen of the Amazons, betrothed to Theseus
HERMIA, daughter to Egeus, in love with Lysander
HELENA, in love with Demetrius
OBERON, King of the fairies
TITANIA, Queen of the fairies
PUCK, or Robin Goodfellow
PEASEBLOSSOM
COBWEB
MOTH } fairies
MUSTARDSEED

Other fairies attending their King and Queen. Attendants
on Theseus and Hippolyta

SCENE *Athens, and a wood nearby*

Theseus, Duke of Athens, and Hippolyta are to be married in four days' time and are looking forward to the wedding. They want the whole of Athens to celebrate. Egeus, Hermia's father, arrives.

our nuptial … apace: our wedding day will soon be here

four happy … moon: in four days' time a new month begins

methinks: it seems to me

lingers: delays

stepdame: stepmother

dowager: widow

withering out: wasting away

revenue: income. Theseus has to wait for his wedding-day just as a young man who inherits his father's money may have to wait to enjoy it all himself, because his mother or stepmother still has to use some of it.

steep themselves: be absorbed, lose themselves

behold: see

solemnities: celebrations

pert and nimble: lively and quick, agile

forth: out

pomp: procession, pageant. Sadness is not suitable for our festivities

Hippolyta … injuries: Theseus beat the Amazons in battle. Hippolyta was their queen.

triumph: celebration(s)

revelling: entertainment

Act one

Athens

Enter THESEUS, HIPPOLYTA, PHILOSTRATE, *and* ATTENDANTS

THESEUS | Now, fair Hippolyta, our nuptial hour
Draws on apace. Four happy days bring in
Another moon. But, O, methinks, how slow
This old moon wanes, she lingers my desires,
Like to a step-dame or a dowager,
Long withering out a young man's revenue.

HIPPOLYTA | Four days will quickly steep themselves in night,
Four nights will quickly dream away the time;
And then the moon, like to a silver bow
New-bent in heaven, shall behold the night   10
Of our solemnities.

THESEUS | Go Philostrate,
Stir up the Athenian youth to merriments,
Awake the pert and nimble spirit of mirth,
Turn melancholy forth to funerals;
The pale companion is not for our pomp.

[*Exit Philostrate*

Hippolyta, I wooed thee with my sword,
And won thy love, doing thee injuries.
But I will wed thee in another key,
With pomp, with triumph, and with revelling.

Enter EGEUS, HERMIA, LYSANDER, *and* DEMETRIUS

EGEUS | Happy be Theseus, our renowned duke.   20

THESEUS | Thanks good Egeus. What's the news with thee?

Egeus complains to Theseus that Hermia is refusing to marry Demetrius, who is her father's choice for her, and instead is in love with Lysander and wants to marry him. Athenian law states she must either give in to her father's wishes or face the death penalty or spend the rest of her life in a convent.

vexation: annoyance

bewitched ... child: charmed my daughter's heart

love-tokens: little presents given as a sign of love

feigning voice ... feigning love: in a voice pretending to be sincere, a love that was not

stolen ... fantasy: captured her imagination in a sly way

gauds, conceits: toys and trinkets

Knacks: knick-knacks

trifles: toys or trinkets

nosegays: posies or bunches of flowers

sweetmeats: sweet food, such as sugared cakes, candied fruit, sugared nuts etc.

messengers ... youth: gifts which have a lot of power to influence a young girl

filched: stolen

harshness: hostility

Be it so: if

privilege: special right, law

Immediately: expressly

Be advised: consider

To whom ... disfigure it: Theseus suggests that a daughter has been created by her father, and, as though she were a wax model, she can either be left in the finished state or be destroyed by him.

EGEUS   Full of vexation come I, with complaint
Against my child, my daughter Hermia.
Stand forth, Demetrius. My noble lord,
This man hath my consent to marry her.
Stand forth, Lysander. And my gracious duke,
This man hath bewitched the bosom of my child.
Thou, thou, Lysander, thou hast given her rhymes,
And interchanged love-tokens with my child.
Thou hast by moonlight at her window sung,   30
With feigning voice, verses of feigning love,
And stolen the impression of her fantasy
With bracelets of thy hair, rings, gauds, conceits,
Knacks, trifles, nosegays, sweetmeats–messengers
Of strong prevailment in unhardened youth.
With cunning hast thou filched my daughter's heart,
Turned her obedience, which is due to me,
To stubborn harshness. And my gracious duke,
Be it so she will not here before your grace
Consent to marry with Demetrius,   40
I beg the ancient privilege of Athens.
As she is mine, I may dispose of her
Which shall be either to this gentlemen,
Or to her death, according to our law
Immediately provided in that case.

THESEUS   What say you Hermia? Be advised fair maid.
To you your father should be as a god;
One that composed your beauties; yea and one
To whom you are but as a form in wax
By him imprinted, and within his power   50
To leave the figure or disfigure it.
Demetrius is a worthy gentleman.

HERMIA   So is Lysander.

THESEUS   In himself he is,

Hermia is insistent that she would rather become a nun than marry Demetrius. Theseus gives Hermia until his wedding day to decide.

in this kind: in this respect
wanting: lacking
voice: approval, favour
entreat: beg
die the death: be put to death by the state
abjure: renounce. Hermia's choice, if she will not obey her father is to be put to death or to spend the rest of her life as a nun.
blood: passions
question ... blood: Theseus urges her to think hard about her emotions and her needs and to remember that she is young.
yield: give way
livery: costume, habit
aye: ever
mewed: shut up
fruitless moon: the moon goddess Diana, a virgin, the symbol of chastity
master so their blood: control their passions in this way
To ... pilgrimage: To submit themselves to life as a virgin
earthlier happy: happier on earth
the rose distilled: perfume was distilled from roses. Theseus is suggesting that a woman who marries is happier than one who gives everything up to become a nun.
patent: privilege
his lordship: Demetrius as my husband
unwished yoke: unwanted domination/marriage
whose ... sovereignty: She is saying ' My whole being rejects this marriage. I cannot call him my lord and master.'
The sealing-day: the day of Theseus' own marriage
as he would: as your father wants
protest: make a vow

But in this kind, wanting your father's voice,
The other must be held the worthier.

HERMIA I would my father looked but with my eyes.

THESEUS Rather your eyes must with his judgement look.

HERMIA I do entreat your grace to pardon me.
I know not by what power I am made bold,
Nor how it may concern my modesty   60
In such a presence here to plead my thoughts.
But I beseech your grace that I may know
The worst that may befall me in this case,
If I refuse to wed Demetrius.

THESEUS Either to die the death, or to abjure
For ever the society of men.
Therefore, fair Hermia, question your desires,
Know of your youth, examine well your blood,
Whether, if you yield not to your father's choice,
You can endure the livery of a nun,   70
For aye to be in shady cloister mewed,
To live a barren sister all your life,
Chanting faint hymns to the cold fruitless moon.
Thrice-blessed they that master so their blood,
To undergo such maiden pilgrimage.
But earthlier happy is the rose distilled,
Than that which withering on the virgin thorn
Grows, lives, and dies in single blessedness.

HERMIA So will I grow, so live, so die, my lord,
Ere I will yield my virgin patent up   80
Unto his lordship, whose unwished yoke
My soul consents not to give sovereignty.

THESEUS Take time to pause, and, by the next new moon–
The sealing-day betwixt my love and me,
For everlasting bond of fellowship–
Upon that day either prepare to die
For disobedience to your father's will,
Or else to wed Demetrius, as he would,
Or on Diana's altar to protest

Egeus, Demetrius and Lysander argue the case and
Lysander mentions that until recently Demetrius has
been in love with Helena, who is still madly in love
with him.

austerity: self-discipline
relent: change your mind
yield thy crazed title: give up your silly claim
render: give
estate: grant to, settle on
I am ... as he: I am from as good a family as he is
well-possessed: rich
My ... ranked: my possessions are equal to
with vantage: better
prosecute my right: follow-up my claim
avouch it to his head: state it to his face
dotes in idolatry upon: worships as if he were a god
spotted and inconstant: secondhand and changeable.
    Lysander is making it clear that Hermia is not
    Demetrius' first love.

1 Theseus has heard that Demetrius has fallen out of
   love with Helena and in love with Hermia, but he has
   been too preoccupied to speak to him.
2 Now, telling Hermia to choose between death or life in
   a convent by the date of his wedding, he takes Egeus
   and Demetrius aside to have a word with them.

For aye austerity and single life.   90

DEMETRIUS   Relent, sweet Hermia: and, Lysander, yield
Thy crazed title to my certain right.

LYSANDER   You have her father's love, Demetrius;
Let me have Hermia's. Do you marry him.

EGEUS   Scornful Lysander, true, he hath my love,
And what is mine my love shall render him.
And she is mine, and all my right of her
I do estate unto Demetrius.

LYSANDER   I am my lord, as well derived as he,
As well possessed. My love is more than his;   100
My fortunes every way as fairly ranked,
If not with vantage, as Demetrius';
And, which is more than all these boasts can be,
I am beloved of beauteous Hermia.
Why should not I then prosecute my right?
Demetrius, I'll avouch it to his head,
Made love to Nedar's daughter, Helena,
And won her soul; and she, sweet lady, dotes,
Devoutly dotes, dotes in idolatry,
Upon this spotted and inconstant man.   110

THESEUS   I must confess that I have heard so much,
And with Demetrius thought to have spoke thereof;
But being over-full of self-affairs,
My mind did lose it. Demetrius come,
And come Egeus, you shall go with me,
I have some private schooling for you both.
For you fair Hermia, look you arm yourself
To fit your fancies to your father's will;
Or else the law of Athens yields you up–
Which by no means we may extenuate–   120
To death, or to a vow of single life.
Come my Hippolyta, what cheer my love?
Demetrius and Egeus go along,
I must employ you in some business
Against our nuptial, and confer with you

Lysander and Hermia, left alone together, talk about the pleasure and pain of being in love.

3 Lysander and Hermia are left alone together.

3 >

Belike: perhaps

well beteem: easily allow

from the tempest of my eyes: from the storm in my eyes. She is unhappy and near to tears.

For aught: from anything

by tale or history: from talk or from a story

different in blood: (lovers) not of the same social class

O cross! - too high ... low: What a cross to bear! Of too high a rank to be enslaved to a lower one.

misgraffèd: badly matched (by age)

stood upon: depended on

sympathy: agreement

lay siege: lie in wait to attack

momentany: 'momentary' - short-lived, fleeting

collied: blackened, dark

spleen: the part of the body regarded as producing emotions and passions. Here fit or flash of anger

ere: before (Before you can say 'Look at the lightning!' it has gone - lost in the darkness again.)

come to confusion: get destroyed

have been ever crossed: have always met with difficulties

It ... destiny: It has the force of a law in our fate.

Then ... cross: So we must learn to have patience in our difficulties because it is a common hardship.

As due ... as: as natural as

fancy's: love's

persuasion: argument

dowager: a widow who has property from her husband

	Of something nearly that concerns yourselves.
EGEUS	With duty and desire we follow you.

[Exeunt all but Lysander and Hermia

LYSANDER	How now my love? Why is your cheek so pale?
	How chance the roses there do fade so fast?
HERMIA	Belike for want of rain, which I could well 130
	Beteem them from the tempest of my eyes.
LYSANDER	Ay me! For aught that I could ever read,
	Could ever hear by tale or history,
	The course of true love never did run smooth;
	But either it was different in blood–
HERMIA	O cross! Too high to be enthralled to low.
LYSANDER	Or else misgraffed in respect of years–
HERMIA	O spite! Too old to be engaged to young.
LYSANDER	Or else it stood upon the choice of friends–
HERMIA	O hell! To choose love by another's eyes. 140
LYSANDER	Or, if there were a sympathy in choice,
	War, death, or sickness did lay siege to it,
	Making it momentany as a sound,
	Swift as a shadow, short as any dream;
	Brief as the lightning in the collied night,
	That, in a spleen, unfolds both heaven and earth,
	And ere a man hath power to say 'Behold!'
	The jaws of darkness do devour it up.
	So quick bright things come to confusion.
HERMIA	If then true lovers have been ever crossed, 150
	It stands as an edict in destiny.
	Then let us teach our trial patience,
	Because it is a customary cross,
	As due to love, as thoughts and dreams and sighs,
	Wishes and tears, poor fancy's followers.
LYSANDER	A good persuasion. Therefore hear me, Hermia.
	I have a widow aunt, a dowager
	Of great revenue, and she hath no child;

They arrange to meet in the wood the following evening to elope and marry away from Athens and its laws. Helena arrives. She cannot get Demetrius to love her.

league: about 5 kilometres
Steal forth: creep away from
without: outside
To ... May: to carry out the May Day ceremonies
stay: wait

1 Hermia promises Lysander faithfully that she will meet him as he suggests on the the following day to elope with him.
2 They greet Helena.

fair: beautiful
unsay: cancel
fair: (here) kind/type of beauty
lodestars: guiding-stars
your tongue's sweet air: the sound of your words
tuneable: tuneful, musical
favour: good looks
bated: excepted
translated: transformed, changed

From Athens is her house remote seven leagues,
And she respects me as her only son.   160
There, gentle Hermia, may I marry thee;
And to that place the sharp Athenian law
Cannot pursue us. If thou lovest me then,
Steal forth thy father's house tomorrow night,
And in the wood, a league without the town,
Where I did meet thee once with Helena,
To do observance to a morn of May,
There will I stay for thee.

HERMIA   My good Lysander,
I swear to thee by Cupid's strongest bow,
By his best arrow with the golden head,   170
By the simplicity of Venus' doves,
By that which knitteth souls, and prospers loves,
And by that fire which burned the Carthage queen,
When the false Troyan under sail was seen,
By all the vows that ever men have broke,
In number more than ever women spoke,
In that same place thou hast appointed me,
Tomorrow truly will I meet with thee.

LYSANDER   Keep promise love. Look, here comes Helena.

Enter HELENA

HERMIA   God speed fair Helena, whither away?   180

HELENA   Call you me fair? That fair again unsay.
Demetrius loves your fair. O happy fair!
Your eyes are lode-stars, and your tongue's sweet air
More tuneable than lark to shepherd's ear,
When wheat is green, when hawthorn buds appear.
Sickness is catching. O were favour so,
Yours would I catch, fair Hermia, ere I go,
My ear should catch your voice, my eye your eye,
My tongue should catch your tongue's sweet melody.
Were the world mine, Demetrius being bated,   190
The rest I'd give to be to you translated.

Hermia tells Helena she cannot put Demetrius off, whatever she does. Hermia and Lysander tell Helena of their plan to elope.

sway the motion: influence the beating
folly: foolishness
would ... : I wish
fly: run away from
graces: charming qualities

1 Lysander and Hermia tell Helena that they are planning to meet in the wood the following night and together will leave Athens.
2 Hermia says goodbye to her childhood friend and asks for her prayers.
3 Both Hermia and Lysander wish Helena luck with Demetrius.

O teach me how you look, and with what art
You sway the motion of Demetrius' heart.

HERMIA I frown upon him, yet he loves me still.

HELENA O that your frowns would teach my smiles such skill.

HERMIA I give him curses, yet he gives me love.

HELENA O that my prayers could such affection move.

HERMIA The more I hate, the more he follows me.

HELENA The more I love, the more he hateth me.

HERMIA His folly, Helena, is no fault of mine. 200

HELENA None but your beauty; would that fault were mine.

HERMIA Take comfort. He no more shall see my face,
Lysander and myself will fly this place.
Before the time I did Lysander see,
Seemed Athens as a paradise to me.
O then, what graces in my love do dwell,
That he hath turned a heaven unto a hell.

LYSANDER Helen, to you our minds we will unfold
Tomorrow night, when Phoebe doth behold
Her silver visage in the watery glass, 210
Decking with liquid pearl the bladed grass–
A time that lovers' flights doth still conceal–
Through Athens' gates have we devised to steal.

HERMIA And in the wood, where often you and I
Upon faint primrose-beds were wont to lie,
Emptying our bosoms of their counsel sweet,
There my Lysander and myself shall meet;
And thence from Athens turn away our eyes
To seek new friends and stranger companies.
Farewell, sweet playfellow; pray thou for us, 220
And good luck grant thee thy Demetrius.
Keep word Lysander, we must starve our sight
From lovers' food till morrow deep midnight.

LYSANDER I will my Hermia.

[*Exit Hermia*

**Left alone Helena tells of her unhappiness -
Demetrius had loved her till he saw Hermia. She
plans to tell him of the elopement - if she doesn't earn
his thanks at least she'll see him in the wood.**

other some: some others. How much happier some people
can be than others.

will not know: refuses to recognise

errs: goes astray, makes mistakes

doting: foolishly in love

base and vile: low and mean

holding no quantity: badly proportioned

transpose: change, transform

form and dignity: beauty and worth. Helena is saying here
that, looked at with love, even things that are low, mean
and out of proportion will appear full of beauty and
worth.

Love looks ... mind: Love does not depend on what
it can actually see, but what it imagines.

Nor ... taste: Neither does love's mind have even the least
amount of judgment.

figure: represent, are a symbol of

beguiled: deceived

waggish: playful. In the same way that, in fun, boys will
pretend things that are not true, the boy who symbolises
love makes false promises too.

eyne: old version of 'eyes'

hailed down: sent down a hailstorm

intelligence: information

a dear expense: worth the trouble

But herein ... back again: I will add to my torment by at
least seeing Demetrius on the way to the wood and back
again.

Helena adieu.
As you on him, Demetrius dote on you.

[*Exit*

HELENA   How happy some o'er other some can be!
Through Athens I am thought as fair as she.
But what of that? Demetrius thinks not so.
He will not know what all but he do know;
And as he errs, doting on Hermia's eyes,   230
So I, admiring of his qualities.
Things base and vile, holding no quantity,
Love can transpose to form and dignity.
Love looks not with the eyes, but with the mind,
And therefore is winged Cupid painted blind.
Nor hath Love's mind of any judgement taste;
Wings and no eyes figure unheedy haste.
And therefore is Love said to be a child,
Because in choice he is so oft beguiled.
As waggish boys in game themselves forswear,   240
So the boy Love is perjured everywhere.
For ere Demetrius looked on Hermia's eyne,
He hailed down oaths that he was only mine;
And when this hail some heat from Hermia felt,
So he dissolved, and showers of oaths did melt.
I will go tell him of fair Hermia's flight.
Then to the wood will he tomorrow night
Pursue her; and for this intelligence
If I have thanks, it is a dear expense.
But herein mean I to enrich my pain,   250
To have his sight thither and back again.

[*Exit*

The Athenian workmen chosen to act in a play for the royal wedding celebrations meet to be given their parts. Quince, the carpenter, is in charge.

generally: Bottom's mistake for the word meaning 'individually'

scrip: piece of paper with writing on it. Here: what you've got written down

scroll: list

interlude: play

treats on: is about, deals with

grow to a point: get to the main business

Marry: Indeed

Masters: form of address 'Gentlemen...'

spread yourselves: spread out

condole: lament, express grief

Ercles: Hercules, famous in Greek mythology for his great strength and cleverness.

a part to tear a cat in: a part needing violent action and loud, ranting speeches

SCENE **2**

Peter Quince's house

Enter, QUINCE, SNUG, BOTTOM, FLUTE, SNOUT, *and* STARVELING

QUINCE   Is all our company here?

BOTTOM   You were best to call them generally, man by man, according to the scrip.

QUINCE   Here is the scroll of every man's name, which is thought fit, through all Athens, to play in our interlude before the duke and the duchess, on his wedding-day at night.

BOTTOM   First good Peter Quince, say what the play treats on, then read the names of the actors, and so grow to a point.   10

QUINCE   Marry, our play is, 'The most lamentable comedy, and most cruel death of Pyramus and Thisby'.

BOTTOM   A very good piece of work I assure you, and a merry. Now good Peter Quince, call forth your actors by the scroll. Masters, spread yourselves.

QUINCE   Answer as I call you. Nick Bottom the weaver.

BOTTOM   Ready. Name what part I am for, and proceed.

QUINCE   You, Nick Bottom, are set down for Pyramus.

BOTTOM   What is Pyramus? A lover, or a tyrant?

QUINCE   A lover that kills himself most gallant for love.   20

BOTTOM   That will ask some tears in the true performing of it. If I do it, let the audience look to their eyes; I will move storms, I will condole in some measure. To the rest. Yet my chief humour is for a tyrant; I could play Ercles rarely, or a part to tear a cat in, to make all split.

Bottom, the weaver, is the dominant personality and can see himself in every role.

Phibbus' car: the chariot of Phoebus, the sun-god
The Fates: three goddesses with influence over the life and
    death of men and women. The first was there at the
    birth, the second spun out the events of his/her life and
    at the end the third cut the thread of life.
vein: style
condoling: sympathetic
An: if

The raging rocks
And shivering shocks
Shall break the locks
    Of prison gates;   30
And Phibbus' car
Shall shine from far,
And make and mar
    The foolish Fates.

This was lofty. Now name the rest of the players.
This is Ercles' vein, a tyrant's vein. A lover is
more condoling.

QUINCE   Francis Flute the bellows-mender.

FLUTE   Here Peter Quince.

QUINCE   Flute, you must take Thisby on you.   40

FLUTE   What is Thisby? A wandering knight?

QUINCE   It is the lady that Pyramus must love.

FLUTE   Nay faith, let not me play a woman, I have a
              beard coming.

QUINCE   That's all one. You shall play it in a mask, and
              you may speak as small as you will.

BOTTOM   An I may hide my face, let me play Thisby too.
              I'll speak in a monstrous little voice, 'Thisne,
              Thisne'. 'Ah Pyramus, my lover dear, thy Thisby
              dear, and lady dear.'   50

QUINCE   No no; you must play Pyramus, and Flute, you
              Thisby.

BOTTOM   Well, proceed.

QUINCE   Robin Starveling the tailor.

STARVELING   Here Peter Quince.

QUINCE   Robin Starveling, you must play Thisby's mother.
              Tom Snout the tinker.

SNOUT   Here Peter Quince.

QUINCE   You, Pyramus' father; myself, Thisby's father;
              Snug the joiner, you the lion's part. And, I hope,   60

Bottom continues to dominate the discussion, offering a variety of make-up for his part.

extempore: without a script, whenever it seems to fit in
aggravate: 'make worse' - Bottom means 'make quieter'

1 Bottom has seen himself in all the parts given out, and now offers to play his own part, Pyramus, the lover who kills himself for love, in any one of a variety of beards.
2 Quince gives out the scripts and asks his actors to learn them by the following night.

	here is a play fitted.
SNUG	Have you the lion's part written? Pray you, if it be, give it me, for I am slow of study.
QUINCE	You may do it extempore, for it is nothing but roaring.
BOTTOM	Let me play the lion too. I will roar, that I will do any man's heart good to hear me. I will roar, that I will make the duke say, 'Let him roar again, let him roar again'.
QUINCE	An you should do it too terribly, you would fright the duchess, and the ladies, that they would shriek, and that were enough to hang us all. 72
ALL	That would hang us, every mother's son.
BOTTOM	I grant you, friends, if that you should fright the ladies out of their wits, they would have no more discretion but to hang us; but I will aggravate my voice so, that I will roar you as gently as any sucking dove; I will roar you an 'twere any nightingale.
QUINCE	You can play no part but Pyramus, for Pyramus is a sweet-faced man, a proper man as one shall see in a summer's day; a most lovely, gentleman-like man therefore you must needs play Pyramus. 83
BOTTOM	Well, I will undertake it. What beard were I best to play it in?
QUINCE	Why, what you will.
BOTTOM	I will discharge it in either your straw-colour beard, your orange-tawny beard, your purple-in-grain beard, or your French-crown-colour beard, your perfect yellow. 90
QUINCE	Some of your French crowns have no hair at all, and then you will play barefaced. But masters, here are your parts, and I am to entreat you, request you, and desire you, to con them by tomorrow night; and meet me in the palace wood,

They arrange a rehearsal in the wood for the following evening.

3 ▷

3   They arrange to meet in the wood, as Quince wants to keep their rehearsals secret.

ACTIVITIES

Keeping track

Scene 1

1   What is happening at the opening of the play?
2   Who does Hermia wish to marry?
3   Who does her father, Egeus, wish her to marry?
4   What is the penalty Hermia must pay for disobeying her father?
5   Who does Helena love?

Scene 2

6   Why have Quince, Bottom and the others met together?
7   To whom do they hope to perform their tragedy?
8   What do we learn about the play they are going to perform?
9   What do you expect will happen in it?
10 What do you imagine the performance will be like?

a mile without the town, by moonlight; there will we
rehearse. For if we meet in the city, we shall be
dogged with company, and our devices known. In
the meantime I will draw a bill of properties, such as
our play wants. I pray you fail me not.   100

BOTTOM   We will meet, and there we may rehearse most
obscenely and courageously. Take pains, be
perfect. Adieu.

QUINCE   At the duke's oak we meet.

BOTTOM   Enough. Hold or cut bow-strings.

[*Exeunt*

Discussion

Scene 1

1 Egeus bursts in unexpectedly on Theseus and Hippolyta,
complaining that his daughter, Hermia, is refusing to marry
the man of his choice. How do you think the Duke and his
fiancée feel about this?

2 How does Theseus expect Hermia to behave towards her
father (lines 47–51)? What is your view of this?

3 Hermia says, "I know not by what power I am made
bold"(Line 59). Can you suggest what makes her behave as
she does?

4 What do you think of Lysander's plan to run away with
Hermia?

5 Why does Helena decide to tell Demetrius that Hermia, her
best friend, is eloping with Lysander? What are your feelings
about this?

Scene 2

6 What sort of picture of 'ladies' do the workmen have?

Character

1 What is your impression of :
   - Theseus
   - Hippolyta?
2 What sort of man is Egeus?
3 Which of the characters in Scene 2 are troublesome and why?

   Who would be affected by this? Do you notice any signs of irritation in what he says?
4 Do you think that Quince is a good leader? What qualities does he have that make him lead well?

Character logs

Start Character logs for:

Theseus - Hippolyta - Egeus - Hermia - Helena - Lysander - Demetrius - Bottom - Quince

See page 194 for suggestions on how to keep a log.

Close study

Lines 1-19

Theseus announces to the court his forthcoming wedding to Hippolyta.

1 How does he feel about it?
2 What is Hippolyta's response?
3 What mood is created by these opening speeches?

Lines 27-38

Egeus accuses Lysander of using tricks to make Hermia fall in love with him. Make a list of these 'tricks', then add other ways mentioned in Scene 1 that lovers have been drawn to each other.

Drama

Role play

In pairs.

1 Hermia speaks of her long-standing friendship with Helena (lines 214-216). What sort of secrets did the girls share? Try out the conversations they may have had together, in role.

2 Imagine one of the 'rude mechanicals' (workmen) is telling a friend or relative who isn't involved in the production about how the first play meeting went. Play the scene in role.

3 Try out a situation where one person is attempting to sort out a difficult problem and another person is unable to resist interrupting and trying to take over (as Bottom does, when Quince is organising the play).

Photographs

In groups.
Choose five significant moments which sum up what has happened in the first scene of Act 1. Make a photograph of each of these moments. (See page 197 for help on creating photographs.)

Hotseating

Hotseat each of the lovers about their thoughts and feelings at the end of Act 1. (See page 196 for suggestions on hotseating.)
Sample questions:

- Hermia might be asked, "How important is your father to you?"
- Helena might be asked, " Do you honestly feel that Hermia is more attractive than you?"
- Demetrius might be asked, "What do you think about your treatment of Helena?"

Close study

The moon is mentioned several times in Scene 1. Make two columns on your page headed:

Moon references	Mood created

- In the left hand column, write each complete reference from the play. Use quotation marks.
- In the second column, explain what the words describing the moon tell us about the feelings of the characters who speak them, and about their situation.

Writing

1 Hermia writes an anguished letter to an 'agony aunt' in a magazine asking for advice. Write the reply, which puts forward both the pros and cons of arranged marriages.

2 You are a society reporter for the *Athenian Tribune*. You witnessed the scenes at the court and you rush to write your gossip column. Write your story for use on the front page.

3 Lysander promises Hermia that he will arrange their elopement with his aunt. He decides to send a letter on ahead to prepare the way. What does he put in this letter?

4 Demetrius meets a friend after his confrontation with Theseus and Egeus and tells him of his situation. Write their conversation either as a script or as a story (using direct speech).

5 Hermia keeps a diary in which she records her personal thoughts. Write her diary entry before she was taken to the palace, and then the one she writes at the end of this scene.

6 Design a poster advertising the play of *Pyramus and Thisby*. Include the names of the players and the characters they will play.

Quiz

Who said the following and to whom?

1 To you your father should be as a god.
2 The course of true love never did run smooth.
3 Love looks not with the eyes but with the mind
   And therefore is winged Cupid painted blind.
4 Nay, faith, let me not play a woman - I have a beard
   coming.

Puck, who serves Oberon, the Fairy King, and a fairy
who serves Titania, the Fairy Queen, meet. Puck
explains that Oberon will be in the wood that evening
and that he and Titania have quarrelled over the
ownership of a human child.

Puck: devil or imp. Puck is also referred to as Robin
   Goodfellow.
thorough: through
pale: fence
moon's sphere: the orbit of the moon
orbs: fairy rings, circles of darker grass, believed to be
   where fairies danced
pensioners: bodyguards to the king or queen within the
   royal palace, first set up by Henry VIII, and chosen for
   their height
favours: gifts
savours: smells, perfume
lob: clown, lout, country bumpkin
elves: young boy fairies
anon: soon, shortly
Take heed: Take care
passing: exceedingly
fell: fierce, angry
wrath: furious
changeling: usually a child left by fairies in exchange for a
   human child they had stolen, but here the stolen child.
   Titania's story about the boy is different (lines 123-37).
train: followers, attendants
trace: range over, pass through
perforce: by force

Act two

A wood near Athens

Enter a FAIRY *at one door, and* PUCK *at another*

PUCK   How now, spirit, whither wander you?

FAIRY   Over hill, over dale,
Thorough bush, thorough brier,
Over park, over pale,
Thorough flood, thorough fire;
I do wander every where,
Swifter than the moon's sphere;
And I serve the Fairy Queen,
To dew her orbs upon the green.
The cowslips tall her pensioners be,   10
In their gold coats spots you see,
Those be rubies, fairy favours,
In those freckles live their savours.
I must go seek some dewdrops here,
And hang a pearl in every cowslip's ear.
Farewell thou lob of spirits; I'll be gone.
Our queen and all her elves come here anon.

PUCK   The king doth keep his revels here tonight.
Take heed the queen come not within his sight.
For Oberon is passing fell and wrath,   20
Because that she, as her attendant, hath
A lovely boy stolen from an Indian king.
She never had so sweet a changeling.
And jealous Oberon would have the child
Knight of his train, to trace the forests wild.
But she perforce withholds the loved boy,
Crowns him with flowers, and makes him all her joy.
And now they never meet in grove, or green,

The fairy recognises Puck as the imp who plays tricks on humans and amuses his master. Puck describes some of his favourite tricks.

Oberon and Titania meet. Titania makes it clear she does not want to see him, or be with him.

starlight sheen: shining light of the stars
square: quarrel
making: shape, build, form
shrewd: mischievous
villagery: villages
Skim milk: steal the cream
quern: hand-mill for grinding corn
bootless: uselessly (Puck stops the milk being churned into butter)
barm: froth on beer
Hobgoblin: another name for Robin Goodfellow
beguile: trick
gossip: old woman
crab: crab apple
dewlap: loose skin hanging from the neck
aunt: old woman
saddest: most serious
'tailor': tail! or bum! - an exclamation used when someone sits down heavily on the floor.
falls into a cough: has a coughing fit
quire: company
waxen: increase
neeze: sneeze
wasted: spent
room: draw back, make way
hence: away
I have ... company: I have sworn not to share his bed or his company

By fountain clear, or spangled starlight sheen,
But they do square, that all their elves for fear   30
Creep into acorn-cups, and hide them there.

FAIRY   Either I mistake your shape and making quite,
Or else you are that shrewd and knavish sprite
Called Robin Goodfellow. Are not you he,
That frights the maidens of the villagery,
Skim milk, and sometime labour in the quern,
And bootless make the breathless housewife churn,
And sometime make the drink to bear no barm,
Mislead night-wanderers, laughing at their harm?
Those that Hobgoblin call you, and sweet Puck,   40
You do their work, and they shall have good luck.
Are not you he?

PUCK   Thou speak'st aright;
I am that merry wanderer of the night.
I jest to Oberon and make him smile,
When I a fat and bean-fed horse beguile,
Neighing in likeness of a filly foal;
And sometimes lurk I in a gossip's bowl,
In very likeness of a roasted crab,
And when she drinks, against her lips I bob,
And on her withered dewlap pour the ale.   50
The wisest aunt, telling the saddest tale,
Sometimes for three-foot stool mistaketh me;
Then slip I from her bum, down topples she,
And 'tailor' cries, and falls into a cough;
And then the whole quire hold their hips and laugh,
And waxen in their mirth, and neeze, and swear
A merrier hour was never wasted there.
But room, fairy, here comes Oberon.

FAIRY   And here my mistress. Would that he were gone.

*Enter OBERON at one door, with his train; and
TITANIA at another, with hers*

OBERON   Ill met by moonlight, proud Titania.   60

TITANIA   What, jealous Oberon? Fairies, skip hence.
I have forsworn his bed and company.

They accuse one another of having been in love with Hippolyta and Theseus. Their quarrels have caused unseasonal weather.

1 >

1 Titania accuses Oberon of having taken the shape of a shepherd, Corin, to sing of love to Phillida.
2 She also claims that he had loved Hippolyta and has come from India to be at her wedding and to wish the marriage joy and prosperity.

2 >

3 Oberon retorts that she has loved Theseus and has tempted him away from women Theseus had loved and made promises to.

3 >

forgeries: false inventions
middle summer's spring: the beginning of midsummer
mead: meadow
beached margent: shingle sea-shore
ringlets: circular dances or fairy rings
sport: pleasure
contagious: harmful
pelting: little
proud: swollen
overborne their continents: flooded their banks
The ploughman ... beard: The ploughman's work has been made pointless and the young corn plants have rotted in the fields before even producing new ears of corn (barley is said to have a beard)
murrion flock: diseased sheep
nine men's morris: area marked out for an outdoor game, something like draughts. Each player had nine pieces.

OBERON	Tarry, rash wanton. Am not I thy lord?
TITANIA	Then I must be thy lady. But I know

TITANIA   When thou hast stolen away from fairy land,
And in the shape of Corin sat all day,
Playing on pipes of corn, and versing love
To amorous Phillida. Why art thou here,
Come from the farthest steep of India?
But that, forsooth, the bouncing Amazon,   70
Your buskined mistress, and your warrior love,
To Theseus must be wedded; and you come
To give their bed joy and prosperity.

OBERON   How canst thou thus for shame, Titania,
Glance at my credit with Hippolyta,
Knowing I know thy love to Theseus?
Didst thou not lead him through the glimmering
    night
From Perigenia, whom he ravished?
And make him with fair Ægles break his faith,
With Ariadne, and Antiopa?   80

TITANIA   These are the forgeries of jealousy.
And never, since the middle summer's spring,
Met we on hill, in dale, forest, or mead,
By paved fountain, or by rushy brook,
Or in the beached margent of the sea,
To dance our ringlets to the whistling wind,
But with thy brawls thou hast disturbed our sport.
Therefore the winds, piping to us in vain,
As in revenge, have sucked up from the sea
Contagious fogs; which falling in the land,   90
Hath every pelting river made so proud,
That they have overborne their continents.
The ox hath therefore stretched his yoke in vain,
The ploughman lost his sweat, and the green corn
Hath rotted ere his youth attained a beard.
The fold stands empty in the drowned field,
And crows are fatted with the murrion flock;
The nine men's morris is filled up with mud,

Titania continues telling Oberon about the floods in
summer and the roses in winter caused by their
quarrels. Oberon says that she has the power to end
the quarrel but she again refuses to hand over the
child, whose mother was one of her companions.

quaint mazes: complicated pattern of paths, often used,
and so usually easy to see

wanton green: luxuriant grass

want: lack

cheer: entertainments

governess: controller

distemperature: double meaning, 'bad temper' and
'bad weather'

hoary: greyish-white

Hiems: personification of winter

crown: head

chaplet: garland

childing: fertile, fruitful

wonted liveries: usual clothes

mazed: bewildered, confused

increase: products (of the various seasons). Because of
the upsets in the weather it is impossible to tell by
looking at what the seasons produce, which is which.

progeny: children

And this same ... dissension: And these catastrophes
are the result of our quarrel, our disagreement.

original: origin

amend: put it right

It lies in you: you have the power

henchman: page

1 ▷

1 Titania again refuses to part with the child, saying that
his mother was one of her companions, she had taken
a vow to Titania and they enjoyed one another's
company.

And the quaint mazes in the wanton green,
For lack of tread, are undistinguishable.   100
The human mortals want their winter cheer,
No night is now with hymn or carol blest.
Therefore the moon, the governess of floods,
Pale in her anger, washes all the air,
That rheumatic diseases do abound.
And thorough this distemperature we see
The seasons alter; hoary-headed frosts
Fall in the fresh lap of the crimson rose,
And on old Hiems' thin and icy crown
An odorous chaplet of sweet summer buds   110
Is, as in mockery, set. The spring, the summer,
The childing autumn, angry winter, change
Their wonted liveries; and the mazed world,
By their increase, now knows not which is which.
And this same progeny of evils comes
From our debate, from our dissension;
We are their parents and original.

OBERON   Do you amend it then, it lies in you.
Why should Titania cross her Oberon?
I do but beg a little changeling boy,   120
To be my henchman.

TITANIA   Set your heart at rest,
The fairy land buys not the child of me.
His mother was a vot'ress of my order,
And in the spiced Indian air, by night,
Full often hath she gossiped by my side,
And sat with me on Neptune's yellow sands,
Marking th' embarked traders on the flood;
When we have laughed to see the sails conceive,
And grow big-bellied with the wanton wind;
Which she, with pretty and with swimming gait   130
Following, her womb then rich with my young squire,
Would imitate, and sail upon the land,
To fetch me trifles, and return again,
As from a voyage, rich with merchandise.

The boy's mother died in childbirth and because they
had been so close, Titania took the child and is
bringing him up. She will not part with him. When
Titania leaves to avoid a worse quarrel, Oberon vows
to torment her. He reminds Puck of a time when they
saw an arrow from Cupid's bow fall on a flower.

2 When the woman died in childbirth Titania took the
  child and brought him up and for her sake she will not
  give him up to Oberon.
3 In reply to Oberon's question, Titania says that she
  will probably stay in the wood until after Theseus'
  wedding day. If Oberon is prepared to join in the
  dances and celebrations he is welcome. If not, they
  will stay away from each other.
4 Oberon again demands the boy and Titania again
  refuses and leaves.

injury: insult
hither: here (to me)
since: when
dulcet: sweet
rude: rough
civil: calm
fair vestal: beautiful virgin (usually taken to refer to
    Queen Elizabeth I)
love-shaft: Cupid's golden arrow
As it: as if it
I might see: I was able to see
Quenched ... watery moon: Moonbeams put out the
    blazing arrow. Diana, virgin moon-goddess was
    protecting a virgin.
vot'ress: woman who has taken a vow
In maiden ... fancy-free: With innocent thoughts, free
    of love.

But she, being mortal, of that boy did die,
And for her sake do I rear up her boy,
And for her sake I will not part with him.

OBERON   How long within this wood intend you stay?

TITANIA   Perchance till after Theseus' wedding-day.
If you will patiently dance in our round,   140
And see our moonlight revels, go with us;
If not, shun me, and I will spare your haunts.

OBERON   Give me that boy, and I will go with thee.

TITANIA   Not for thy fairy kingdom. Fairies away,
We shall chide downright, if I longer stay.

                    [*Exit Titania with her train*

OBERON   Well, go thy way. Thou shalt not from this grove.
Till I torment thee for this injury.
My gentle Puck come hither. Thou remembrest
Since once I sat upon a promontory,
And heard a mermaid, on a dolphin's back,   150
Uttering such dulcet and harmonious breath,
That the rude sea grew civil at her song,
And certain stars shot madly from their spheres,
To hear the sea-maid's music.

PUCK   I remember.

OBERON   That very time I saw–but thou couldst not–
Flying between the cold moon and the earth,
Cupid all armed. a certain aim he took
At a fair vestal, throned by the west,
And loosed his love-shaft smartly from his bow,
As it should pierce a hundred thousand hearts: 160
But I might see young Cupid's fiery shaft
Quenched in the chaste beams of the watery moon,
And the imperial vot'ress passed on,
In maiden meditation, fancy-free.
Yet marked I where the bolt of Cupid fell.
It fell upon a little western flower,
Before, milk-white; now purple with love's wound,

The juice of this plant squeezed on the eyelids of a
sleeping person will make him or her fall madly in
love with the first creature seen on awaking. Oberon
will use this to torment Titania and blackmail her
into giving up the child - he can cure her with
another herb. Oberon, invisible, watches Helena
following Demetrius around begging for his love.
Demetrius is looking for Lysander so that he can kill
him and makes it clear he can't stand Helena.

---

love-in-idleness: pansy or heart's ease
leviathan: sea-monster, whale
put a girdle ... earth: make a circuit of the world
conference: conversation
were stolen: had come secretly
and wood: and mad. This was a play on words, possible in
the language of Shakespeare's time.
adamant: imaginary stone or very hard mineral, supposed
to act like a magnet
Leave you ... and I: If you leave off ... I ...

And maidens call it, love-in-idleness.
Fetch me that flower; the herb I showed thee once.
The juice of it on sleeping eyelids laid,   170
Will make or man or woman madly dote
Upon the next live creature that it sees.
Fetch me this herb, and be thou here again
Ere the leviathan can swim a league.

PUCK   I'll put a girdle round about the earth
          In forty minutes.

                                                  [*Exit*

OBERON   Having once this juice,
          I'll watch Titania when she is asleep,
          And drop the liquor of it in her eyes.
          The next thing then she waking looks upon,
          Be it on lion, bear, or wolf, or bull,   180
          On meddling monkey or on busy ape,
          She shall pursue it with the soul of love.
          And ere I take this charm from off her sight—
          As I can take it with another herb—
          I'll make her render up her page to me.
          But who comes here? I am invisible,
          And I will overhear their conference.

          Enter DEMETRIUS, HELENA *following him*

DEMETRIUS I love thee not, therefore pursue me not.
          Where is Lysander, and fair Hermia?
          The one I'll slay, the other slayeth me.   190
          Thou told'st me they were stolen unto this wood;
          And here am I, and wood within this wood,
          Because I cannot meet my Hermia.
          Hence, get thee gone, and follow me no more.

HELENA   You draw me, you hard-hearted adamant;
          But yet you draw not iron, for my heart
          Is true as steel. Leave you your power to draw,
          And I shall have no power to follow you.

Helena is so desperate for Demetrius to love her that she suggests she would he happy to be his dog, even if he kicked and neglected her. He tells her she is stupid to risk her reputation in the forest at night; he says he is sick at the sight of her; he threatens to leave her to the wild animals. Nothing he says or does can get rid of her.

speak you fair: speak kindly to you

give me leave: permit me

impeach: discredit

You ... virginity: Demetrius says 'You call into question your modesty by leaving the city and putting yourself in the hands of someone who doesn't love you; by trusting your virginity, which is so precious, to the possibilities offered by night and the evil influence of a lonely place.'

Your virtue ... privilege: It is your good qualities which make my circumstance favourable.

For that: because

in my respect: to my mind

brakes: bushes

Apollo ... chase: Daphne, running away from Apollo, was changed into a laurel bush to escape from him.

griffin: legendary animal, half lion, half eagle

hind: doe

DEMETRIUS Do I entice you? Do I speak you fair?
Or rather do I not in plainest truth   200
Tell you I do not, nor I cannot love you?

HELENA And even for that do I love you the more.
I am your spaniel; and, Demetrius,
The more you beat me, I will fawn on you.
Use me but as your spaniel, spurn me, strike me,
Neglect me, lose me; only give me leave,
Unworthy as I am, to follow you.
What worser place can I beg in your love,–
And yet a place of high respect with me–
Than to be used as you use your dog?   210

DEMETRIUS Tempt not too much the hatred of my spirit,
For I am sick when I do look on thee.

HELENA And I am sick when I look not on you.

DEMETRIUS You do impeach your modesty too much,
To leave the city, and commit yourself
Into the hands of one that loves you not,
To trust the opportunity of night,
And the ill counsel of a desert place,
With the rich worth of your virginity.

HELENA Your virtue is my privilege. For that   220
It is not night when I do see your face,
Therefore I think I am not in the night;
Nor doth this wood lack worlds of company,
For you in my respect are all the world.
Then how can it be said I am alone,
When all the world is here to look on me?

DEMETRIUS I'll run from thee, and hide me in the brakes,
And leave thee to the mercy of wild beasts.

HELENA The wildest hath not such a heart as you.
Run when you will. The story shall be changed: 230
Apollo flies, and Daphne holds the chase;
The dove pursues the griffin; the mild hind
Makes speed to catch the tiger. Bootless speed,
When cowardice pursues, and valour flies.

Demetrius goes off, threatening to harm Helena if she persists in following him. She does go after him however. When Puck returns with the flower, Oberon takes it for Titania and, having taken pity on Helena, tells Puck to put some on the eyelids of a young man.

stay: wait for
Fie: an exclamation of disgust
Your wrongs ... sex: the wrongs you do me are making me act in a way that disgraces my sex
nymph: a young and beautiful woman
oxlip: a cross between cowslip and primrose. It looks like a large cowslip.
woodbine: honeysuckle
musk-roses: wild roses
eglantine: sweet-briar rose
sometime: for some part of
throws: throws off, casts, sloughs
Weed: garment
espies: catches sight of

DEMETRIUS I will not stay thy questions, let me go.
Or if thou follow me, do not believe
But I shall do thee mischief in the wood.

[Exit Demetrius

HELENA Ay, in the temple, in the town, the field,
You do me mischief. Fie Demetrius,
Your wrongs do set a scandal on my sex.   240
We cannot fight for love, as men may do;
We should be wooed, and were not made to woo.
I'll follow thee, and make a heaven of hell,
To die upon the hand I love so well.

[Exit Helena

OBERON Fare thee well nymph. Ere he do leave this grove,
Thou shalt fly him, and he shall seek thy love.

Enter PUCK

Hast thou the flower there? Welcome wanderer.
PUCK Ay, there it is.
OBERON   I pray thee give it me.
I know a bank where the wild thyme blows,
Where oxlips and the nodding violet grows,   250
Quite over-canopied with luscious woodbine,
With sweet musk-roses, and with eglantine.
There sleeps Titania sometime of the night,
Lulled in these flowers with dances and delight.
And there the snake throws her enamelled skin,
Weed wide enough to wrap a fairy in.
And with the juice of this I'll streak her eyes,
And make her full of hateful fantasies.
Take thou some of it, and seek through this grove:
A sweet Athenian lady is in love   260
With a disdainful youth. Anoint his eyes,
But do it when the next thing he espies
May be the lady. Thou shalt know the man

Puck will know the man Oberon has in mind because he will be wearing Athenian clothes. Puck must carry out his instructions carefully.

Effect it: carry it out
fond on: in love with, infatuated with

CTIVITIES

Keeping track

1 Which characters open this scene and where is it set?
2 Who are Oberon and Titania?
3 What errands does Oberon ask Puck to do?
4 Why is Helena chasing Demetrius through the woods at night?

Discussion

1 What has annoyed Oberon? Do you feel this is justified?
2 Why is Titania angry with him? Is she behaving reasonably?
3 What do you think about Oberon's proposed revenge on Titania? Is he within his rights to treat her like this?

Drama

In groups of three.
If you were directing this scene how would you help the actors to portray these characters of Puck and the fairy? (See Forum theatre on page 198 for further help with this activity.)
1 Read lines 1-58 through on your own.

> By the Athenian garments he hath on.
> Effect it with some care, that he may prove
> More fond on her than she upon her love.
> And look thou meet me ere the first cock crow.

PUCK   Fear not my lord, your servant shall do so.

[*Exeunt*

2 One person should take the role of director, with the other two playing Puck and the fairy.
3 Read the lines through in character.
4 Now discuss these points between you all:
   ● How might the characters move?
   ● Would both characters be the same or contrasting?
   ● How would their voices sound?
   ● How could they show they are different from humans?
5 Now try the scene again using your ideas, with the director as an 'outside eye' to say what is effective and what needs more thought or discussion.

Character

1 What does Puck seem like from the fairy's description of some of his misdeeds? What are his magical qualities?
2 How do Oberon and Titania behave towards each other?
3 Does Oberon have any good qualities?
4 How do you think Helena feels during this scene? What do you feel about her behaviour towards Demetrius?
5 Demetrius says he'll abandon Helena to 'the mercy of wild beasts'. What do you feel about his treatment of her?
6 Add to your Character logs for Puck, Oberon, Titania, Demetrius and Helena.

7 Compare the people that the fairy and Puck talk about with those that Oberon and Titania mention. How do they differ and why do you think Shakespeare has made these differences?

Close study

Dramatic structure

In the Elizabethan theatre actors had to enter and leave the stage without the benefit of scenery and special effects. Read through this scene again, writing down:
● the opening lines characters use
● when and how they introduce other characters
● the exit lines they use to help them leave the stage
● any other ways they tell the audience what is happening.

Act 2 scene 1 Lines 81-121

Oberon and Titania have power over nature. Look at Titania's speech and make a list of the effects that Oberon's and Titania's quarrel have on human beings and the world. What do you notice about the language she uses?

Lines 188 - 244

Read these lines through with a partner.
Helena and Demetrius are expressing quite different feelings towards each other.
Select those lines which seem to sum up these feelings and write them down under the headings of 'Helena' and 'Demetrius'.
What differences do you notice in the language they use?
What impression does this create of them as individuals?

Lines 188 - 226

Pick out Helena's statements about how her love for Demetrius affects her.

Lines 229 - 244

What comments does Helena make which express her view of how women ought to behave?

Writing

1 We've read on page 59 some of the things Puck does. Think up a trick that Puck might play on either:
   - a modern school teacher
   - a shop keeper
   - or a business person. Describe the incident from the point of view of either the human victim or Puck.

2 Titania pours out her innermost thoughts and feelings to a wise and close friend, about the row with Oberon. Imagine you are Titania and write what she says.

3 Imagine Helena's sister or friend being given a tape of lines 202-210. What advice would she give Helena? In pairs, write it as a script, or, on your own, write it as a letter.

4 In pairs, you are two fairies talking about the events you have witnessed between Oberon and Titania in the wood. Decide whether you are both on the same side, and if so, which, and then script the conversation.

Quiz

Who says:

1 The King doth keep his revels here tonight.
2 Ill-met by moonlight.
3 These are the forgeries of jealousy.
4 I am your spaniel.
5 I am sick when I do look on thee.
6 I'll put a girdle round about the earth in forty minutes.

Titania gives her fairies their tasks for the night and then they sing her a lullaby.

1 Titania organises her fairies for the night. Some are to kill the worms that destroy rosebuds; some to fight the bats for their wings which will be used to make elves' coats, and some are to chase away the owls, which disturb Titania. First they must sing her to sleep.

2 The song is a kind of charm to keep away snakes, newts, slow worms and spiders.

SCENE **2**

The wood

Enter TITANIA, *with her train*

TITANIA   Come, now a roundel and a fairy song;
Then, for the third part of a minute, hence–
Some to kill cankers in the musk-rose buds,
Some war with rere-mice for their leathern wings,
To make my small elves coats, and some keep back
The clamorous owl, that nightly hoots and wonders
At our quaint spirits. Sing me now asleep;
Then to your offices, and let me rest.

Fairies sing

FIRST FAIRY
You spotted snakes with double tongue,
Thorny hedgehogs, be not seen,   10
Newts and blind-worms do no wrong,
Come not near our Fairy Queen.
Philomel, with melody,
Sing in our sweet lullaby,
Lulla, lulla, lullaby, lulla, lulla, lullaby;
    Never harm,
    Nor spell, nor charm,
Come our lovely lady nigh.
So good night, with lullaby.

When the lullaby is over, one fairy stays on guard and the rest leave. Titania falls asleep and Oberon comes in and squeezes the juice on Titania's eyelids. He hopes she will fall in love with a monster.
Oberon leaves and Hermia and Lysander come in. They have lost their way and are exhausted. They plan to sleep until daylight.

3 As her fairies end their song Titania falls asleep. The fairies leave one of their number to stand guard.

4 Oberon, who is invisible, comes in with the flower Puck has brought him. He squeezes the juice on Titania's eyes saying he hopes she will fall in love with a lynx, bear, leopard or boar, or some other horrible creature.

5 Oberon leaves and Lysander and Hermia enter, having lost their way in the wood. They are very tired and decide to lie down and sleep until morning.

SECOND FAIRY
Weaving spiders come not here;   20
   Hence you long-legged spinners, hence.
Beetles black approach not near;
   Worm nor snail, do no offence.
   Philomel, with melody, &c.

FIRST FAIRY
Hence away, now all is well.
One aloof stand sentinel.

              [Exeunt Fairies. Titania sleeps

Enter OBERON, *and squeezes the flower on* TITANIA'S
eyelids

OBERON
    What thou seest when thou dost wake,
    Do it for thy true-love take;
    Love and languish for his sake.
    Be it ounce, or cat, or bear,   30
    Pard, or boar with bristled hair,
    In thy eye that shall appear
    When thou wakest, it is thy dear.
    Wake when some vile thing is near.

                    [Exit

Enter LYSANDER *and* HERMIA

LYSANDER
    Fair love, you faint with wandering in the wood,
    And to speak troth I have forgot our way.
    We'll rest us Hermia, if you think it good,
    And tarry for the comfort of the day.
HERMIA
    Be it so Lysander; find you out a bed,
    For I upon this bank will rest my head.   40
LYSANDER
    One turf shall serve as pillow for us both,
    One heart, one bed, two bosoms, and one troth.
HERMIA
    Nay good Lysander, for my sake, my dear.
    Lie further off yet, do not lie so near.
LYSANDER
    O take the sense, sweet, of my innocence.

Lysander and Hermia lie down some way apart, at her insistence, and they fall asleep. Puck comes along, looking for Demetrius and assumes, as these two lovers are so far apart, that they must be Demetrius and Helena.

6 Hermia insists, out of modesty, that they sleep some distance apart. Lysander does as she asks, and they settle down to sleep.

7 When Puck comes looking for the man Oberon means him to treat with the juice (Demetrius) he assumes, since Lysander is wearing Athenian clothes and is not lying near the woman, that he is the man.

Love takes the meaning in love's conference.
I mean that my heart unto yours is knit,
So that but one heart we can make of it.
Two bosoms interchained with an oath;
So then two bosoms, and a single troth.   50
Then by your side no bed-room me deny;
For lying so, Hermia, I do not lie.

HERMIA   Lysander riddles very prettily.
Now much beshrew my manners and my pride,
If Hermia meant to say Lysander lied.
But gentle friend, for love and courtesy
Lie further off, in human modesty;
Such separation as may well be said
Becomes a virtuous bachelor and a maid,
So far be distant; and good night sweet friend.   60
Thy love ne'er alter till thy sweet life end.

LYSANDER   Amen, amen, to that fair prayer, say I;
And then end life when I end loyalty.
Here is my bed; sleep give thee all his rest.

HERMIA   With half that wish the wisher's eyes be pressed.
                                            [*They sleep*

        Enter PUCK

PUCK   Through the forest have I gone,
                But Athenian found I none,
                On whose eyes I might approve
                This flower's force in stirring love.
                Night and silence–Who is here?   70
                Weeds of Athens he doth wear.
                This is he, my master said,
                Despised the Athenian maid.
                And here the maiden, sleeping sound,
                On the dank and dirty ground.
                Pretty soul, she durst not lie
                Near this lack-love, this kill-courtesy.
                Churl, upon thy eyes I throw

Puck treats Lysander with the magic juice and goes to
report back to Oberon.

Demetrius and Helena come running in. She is still
trying to attract him, but he runs off. She comes to
the conclusion that she must be ugly and can never
compare with Hermia. Suddenly she sees Lysander
on the ground and wakes him up. Of course he
instantly falls in love with her.

8

8 Puck squeezes the juice on Lysander's eyelids.

I charge thee hence: I'm telling you to go away
darkling: in the dark
on thy peril: at your own risk
fond: foolish
grace: answer to a prayer
no marvel though: it's not surprising that
dissembling: deceitful
sphery eyne: star-like eyes
Transparent: bright/beautiful; and also something that can
  be seen through
art: magic power

[Puts the juice on Lysander's eyelids

All the power this charm doth owe.
When thou wakest, let love forbid   80
Sleep his seat on thy eyelid.
So awake when I am gone;
For I must now to Oberon.   *[Exit*

Enter DEMETRIUS *and* HELENA, *running*

HELENA	Stay, though thou kill me, sweet Demetrius.
DEMETRIUS	I charge thee hence, and do not haunt me thus.
HELENA	O wilt thou darkling leave me? Do not so.
DEMETRIUS	Stay, on thy peril; I alone will go. *[Exit*
HELENA	O, I am out of breath in this fond chase.

The more my prayer, the lesser is my grace.
Happy is Hermia, wheresoe'er she lies;   90
For she hath blessed and attractive eyes.
How came her eyes so bright? Not with salt tears;
If so, my eyes are oftener washed than hers.
No, no, I am as ugly as a bear,
For beasts that meet me run away for fear.
Therefore no marvel though Demetrius
Do, as a monster, fly my presence thus.
What wicked and dissembling glass of mine
Made me compare with Hermia's sphery eyne?
But who is here? Lysander, on the ground,   100
Dead, or asleep? I see no blood, no wound.
Lysander, if you live, good sir awake.

LYSANDER   *[Awaking]* And run through fire I will for thy sweet
                  sake.
Transparent Helena, Nature shows art,
That through thy bosom makes me see thy heart.
Where is Demetrius? O how fit a word
Is that vile name to perish on my sword.

HELENA   Do not say so, Lysander, say not so.

Lysander tells Helena he now loves her and not Hermia. Helena thinks he is mocking her, but he insists she is the only one for him. When Helena goes, Lysander leaves Hermia sleeping on the ground and follows, saying he now hates Hermia.

What though: What if

raven: Hermia is often referred to as being 'dark' and Helena as 'fair'

The will ... swayed: We know, and Lysander does not, that magic and not reason has changed his affections.

will: desire

ripe not: have not ripened

And ... skill: And now that I am reaching the high point of my capabilities

marshal to my will: guide for my desires

o'erlook: read

keen: bitter

flout: jeer at, scoff at

insufficiency: inadequacy

Good troth ... good sooth: both mean 'truly', 'indeed'

gentleness: courteous behaviour

of: by

a surfeit: excess, too much

as the heresies ... deceive: as the heresies (false beliefs) that men reject are hated most by those who were once taken in by them

address: direct

What though he love your Hermia? Lord, what
  though?
Yet Hermia still loves you; then be content. 110

LYSANDER Content with Hermia? No, I do repent
The tedious minutes I with her have spent.
Not Hermia, but Helena I love.
Who will not change a raven for a dove?
The will of man is by his reason swayed;
And reason says you are the worthier maid.
Things growing are not ripe until their season;
So I, being young, till now ripe not to reason;
And touching now the point of human skill,
Reason becomes the marshal to my will, 120
And leads me to your eyes, where I o'erlook
Love's stories, written in love's richest book.

HELENA Wherefore was I to this keen mockery born?
When at your hands did I deserve this scorn?
Is't not enough, is't not enough, young man,
That I did never, no nor never can,
Deserve a sweet look from Demetrius' eye,
But you must flout my insufficiency?
Good troth you do me wrong, good sooth you do,
In such disdainful manner me to woo. 130
But fare you well; perforce I must confess
I thought you lord of more true gentleness.
O, that a lady, of one man refused,
Should of another therefore be abused. [*Exit*

LYSANDER She sees not Hermia. Hermia, sleep thou there,
And never mayst thou come Lysander near.
For as a surfeit of the sweetest things
The deepest loathing to the stomach brings;
Or as the heresies that men do leave
Are hated most of those they did deceive; 140
So thou, my surfeit and my heresy,
Of all be hated; but the most of me.
And all my powers address your love and might,

Lysander leaves to follow Helena. Hermia wakes up from a nightmare in which a snake seemed to be eating her heart while Lysander watched, smiling. She calls for Lysander and then realises that he has gone. Still in terror from the dream she goes off to try and find him.

Ay me, for pity!: An exclamation
Methought: I thought
prey: preying
swoon: faint
Then I will perceive: Now I realise
nigh: near

ACTIVITIES

Keeping track

1 What does Titania ask her fairies to do at the opening of this scene?
2 When she is sleeping, what does Oberon do?
3 Why are Hermia and Lysander in the woods at night?
4 Puck makes a mistake in following out Oberon's orders. What is it?
5 What brings Helena to the woods and who does she meet?
6 Who is on stage alone at the scene's end?

Discussion

1 Because Titania won't let Oberon have the changeling boy, he takes revenge on her, when she is asleep. What

	To honour Helen and to be her knight. [*Exit*
HERMIA	[*Awaking*] Help me Lysander, help me; do thy best

To pluck this crawling serpent from my breast.
Ay me, for pity! What a dream was here!
Lysander look how I do quake with fear.
Methought a serpent eat my heart away,
And you sat smiling at his cruel prey.   150
Lysander! What, removed? Lysander, lord!
What, out of hearing, gone? No sound, no word?
Alack where are you? Speak, an if you hear.
Speak, of all loves! I swoon almost with fear.
No? Then I will perceive you are not nigh;
Either death or you I'll find immediately.

[*Exit*

do you think about his behaviour?

2 *A Midsummer Night's Dream* is called a comedy. Are there any sections of this scene which can be performed to make the audience laugh?

3 Hermia has agreed to elope with Lysander. What do you think about how she treats him in this section? What are your views on how he treats her?

Drama

… the patience of a saint …

In pairs.

Demetrius has lost patience with Helena and brushes her off rudely.

Improvise a scene in which one of you persists in making

demands until the other is pushed to the point of losing their temper, for example:

- a young child to its mother
- a teenager to a parent
- a salesman to a potential customer
- a couple of young people at a disco.

Lines 88-110 or 111 -144

Groups of 4.

1 Read through lines 88 –144 on your own.
2 Form pairs and decide which pair will take which lines (88 –110 or 111 –144).
3 Cast the parts and work in pairs.
4 Read through your lines aloud with your partner.
5 Discuss how the lines might be spoken; who is angry, who is consumed with passion.
6 Decide what actions might accompany the words.
7 'Walk' through the scene.
8 Practise it until it seems to work.
9 Join with the other pair and perform the whole scene.

Character

1 It is said that people's true character is shown at times of stress. Here, we see Helena and then Hermia in difficult situations, in a wood at night. What similarities and differences do they show?
2 Lysander speaks about love a great deal. What do we learn about him from what he says?
3 What impression do you get of Demetrius from the brief words he speaks to Helena (lines 91-93)?
4 Bring your Character logs for Lysander, Hermia, Demetrius and Helena up to date.

Close study

Lines 41-52 and lines 103-122

Love is often said to come from the heart.
Look at how Lysander uses images of the heart to win love -
first with Hermia, then with Helena. Make a list of them.

Lines 108-110 and 123-134

In your own words, explain how Helena reacts to Lysander's
promises of love. What accusations does she make against him?

Writing

1 Look at Oberon's spell (lines 27-34) and rewrite it in
   modern English. You can change the beasts, which Oberon
   suggests, to things which are modern monsters.
2 Write Hermia's diary entry after these particular
   happenings in the woods.
3 As Lysander, write to a friend telling him how you had felt
   about Hermia and how you feel about her now. Include
   your feelings about your love for Helena.
4 Prepare a comic strip, in not more than ten frames, of the
   action of this scene.

Quiz

1 In the fairy world, what material are elves' coats made
   from?
2 Who makes a wish, 'Wake when some vile thing is near'?
3 Who says, and to whom 'Lie further off yet'?
4 Name two birds mentioned in this scene.
5 Why should bears feel insulted by Helena?
6 Who says, and to whom? 'And run through fire I will for
   thy sweet sake!'

As Titania lies asleep, invisible, the workmen come in
to start their rehearsal. Bottom is concerned that the
ladies of the court will not be able to stand the sight of
Pyramus killing himself. They agree to write a
reassuring prologue. There is then the further worry
that the ladies will be afraid of the lion.

Are we all met?: Are we all here?
Pat: on the dot
hawthorn brake: hawthorn bush
tiring-house: dressing room. In the Elizabethan theatre it
    would be directly behind the stage.
bully: my friend
By'r lakin: by our Lady
parlous: dreadful, shocking
Not a whit: Not a bit
eight and six: lines of eight and six syllables

Act three

The wood

TITANIA *lying asleep*
Enter QUINCE, SNUG, BOTTOM, FLUTE, SNOUT, *and*
STARVELING

BOTTOM	Are we all met?
QUINCE	Pat, pat; and here's a marvellous convenient place for our rehearsal. This green plot shall be our stage, this hawthorn-brake our tiring-house, and we will do it in action, as we will do it before the duke.
BOTTOM	Peter Quince.
QUINCE	What sayest thou, bully Bottom?
BOTTOM	There are things in this comedy of Pyramus and Thisby that will never please. First, Pyramus must draw a sword to kill himself; which the ladies cannot abide. How answer you that?
SNOUT	By 'r lakin, a parlous fear.
STARVELING	I believe we must leave the killing out, when all is done.
BOTTOM	Not a whit, I have a device to make all well. Write me a prologue, and let the prologue seem to say, we will do no harm with our swords, and that Pyramus is not killed indeed. And, for the more better assurance, tell them that I Pyramus am not Pyramus, but Bottom the weaver; this will put them out of fear.
QUINCE	Well, we will have such a prologue, and it shall be written in eight and six.
BOTTOM	No, make it two more; let it be written in eight and eight.
SNOUT	Will not the ladies be afeard of the lion?
STARVELING	I fear it, I promise you.

10

20

They decide to explain that the lion is really Snug the joiner. The next problem is how to show it is moonlight indoors. They decide one of them must act the moon. They need a wall as well.

Nay: no
defect: Bottom means 'effect'
it were pity ... life: my life would be at risk
chamber: room
almanac: calendar
casement: window
Great Chamber: state room
bush of thorns: traditionally carried by the man in the moon
disfigure: represent

BOTTOM Masters, you ought to consider with yourselves—
to bring in, God shield us, a lion among ladies, is
a most dreadful thing. For there is not a more 30
fearful wild-fowl than your lion living; and we
ought to look to 't.

SNOUT Therefore another prologue must tell he is not a lion.

BOTTOM Nay, you must name his name, and half his face
must be seen through the lion's neck, and he himself
must speak through, saying thus, or to the same
defect 'Ladies,' or 'Fair ladies, I would wish you,' or,
'I would request you,' or, 'I would entreat you, not
to fear, not to tremble; my life for yours. If you think
I come hither as a lion, it were pity of my life. No, I 40
am no such thing, I am a man as other men are;'
and there indeed let him name his name, and tell
them plainly he is Snug the joiner.

QUINCE Well, it shall be so. But there is two hard things; that
is, to bring the moonlight into a chamber; for you
know, Pyramus and Thisby meet by moonlight.

SNOUT Doth the moon shine that night we play our play?

BOTTOM A calendar, a calendar, look in the almanac; find
out moonshine, find out moonshine.

QUINCE Yes, it doth shine that night. 50

BOTTOM Why then may you leave a casement of the great
chamber window, where we play, open, and the
moon may shine in at the casement.

QUINCE Ay, or else one must come in with a bush of
thorns and a lanthorn, and say he comes to
disfigure, or to present, the person of
moonshine. Then, there is another thing we
must have a wall in the great chamber, for
Pyramus and Thisby, says the story, did talk
through the chink of a wall. 60

SNOUT You can never bring in a wall. What say you
Bottom?

They decide one of them must be the wall. They get ready to rehearse. Puck, who is invisible to humans, comes in and decides to watch, and take part if he feels like it. Quince starts to run his rehearsal.

hempen home-spuns: country bumpkins (hemp when spun and woven produced a rough cloth)

toward: in preparation

auditor: listener

odious savours sweet: Bottom has got the wrong word again. 'Odious' means unpleasant whereas all three words - *odorous, savours* and *sweet* - imply scented, sweet-smelling, perfumed.

marry: indeed, to be sure

brisky juvenal: lively youth

eke: also

Jew: it seems to be just a handy ending to rhyme with 'hue'

Ninny: fool. Pyramus and Thisby are to meet at Ninus' tomb. He was the mythical founder of the city of Nineveh.

BOTTOM   Some man or other must present wall: and let
          him have some plaster, or some loam, or some
          rough-cast about him to signify wall; and let him
          hold his fingers thus, and through that cranny
          shall Pyramus and Thisby whisper.

QUINCE   If that may be, then all is well. Come, sit down,
          every mother's son, and rehearse your parts.
          Pyramus, you begin. When you have spoken   70
          your speech, enter into that brake; and so every
          one according to his cue.

          Enter PUCK

PUCK   What hempen home-spuns have we swaggering
              here,
          So near the cradle of the Fairy Queen?
          What, a play toward! I'll be an auditor,
          An actor too perhaps, if I see cause.

QUINCE   Speak, Pyramus, Thisby stand forth.

BOTTOM   Thisby, the flowers of odious savours sweet–

QUINCE   Odours, odours.

BOTTOM   –odours savours sweet,   80
          So hath thy breath, my dearest Thisby dear.
          But hark, a voice; stay thou but here awhile,
          And by and by I will to thee appear.   [*Exit*

PUCK   A stranger Pyramus than e'er played here.   [*Exit*

FLUTE   Must I speak now?

QUINCE   Ay marry, must you. For you must understand
          he goes but to see a noise that he heard, and is to
          come again.   88

FLUTE   Most radiant Pyramus, most lily-white of hue,
          Of colour like the red rose on triumphant briar,
          Most brisky juvenal, and eke most lovely Jew.
          As true as truest horse, that yet would never tire,
          I'll meet thee Pyramus, at Ninny's tomb.

QUINCE   'Ninus' tomb', man. Why you must not speak

Bottom, in his role as the lover, Pyramus, is waiting
for his next cue. When he enters Puck has used his
magic on him and he has an ass's head. His friends
are terrified and rush off. Puck intends to enjoy
himself by leading them a nightmarish dance.
Bottom is bewildered at his friends' reaction, but
decides to sing so they can see he is not afraid.

knavery: silly trick
translated: transformed
ousel cock: male blackbird

that yet; that you answer to Pyramus. You speak
all your part at once, cues and all. Pyramus
enter, your cue is past; it is, 'never tire.'

FLUTE O–as true as truest horse, that yet would never tire.

Enter PUCK, *and* BOTTOM *with an ass's head*

BOTTOM If I were fair, Thisby, I were only thine.

QUINCE O monstrous! O strange! We are haunted. Pray
masters fly, masters! Help!   101

[*Exeunt Quince, Snug, Flute, Snout, and Starveling*

PUCK I'll follow you, I'll lead you about a round,
  Through bog, through bush, through brake,
   through briar.
Sometime a horse I'll be, sometime a hound,
 A hog, a headless bear, sometime a fire.
And neigh, and bark, and grunt, and roar, and burn,
Like horse, hound, hog, bear, fire at every turn.
          [*Exit*

BOTTOM Why do they run away? This is a knavery of
them to make me afeard.   109

Enter SNOUT

SNOUT O Bottom, thou art changed. What do I see on thee?

BOTTOM What do you see? You see an ass-head of your
own, do you?   [*Exit Snout*

Enter QUINCE

QUINCE Bless thee Bottom, bless thee. Thou art translated.
          [*Exit*

BOTTOM I see their knavery. This is to make an ass of me,
to fright me, if they could. But I will not stir from
this place, do what they can. I will walk up and
down here, and I will sing, that they shall hear I
am not afraid.   [*Sings*
  The ousel cock so black of hue,

Bottom's song wakes up Titania, who immediately
falls in love with him. Bottom sings to her and then
says he wants to get out of the wood. She wants him
to stay and can force him to. She promises him
servants from among her fairies.

throstle: thrush

little quill: small piping voice

plain-song cuckoo: the cuckoo which sings a plain tune.
The sound of the cuckoo was by tradition supposed to
sound like 'cuckold' and to be telling husbands that their
wives were deceiving them. This song suggests there are
many men who cannot deny that this has happened.

set his wit: use his intelligence to answer

enamoured of: attracted by

enthralled of: captivated by, delighted by

thy fair virtue's force: the power of your good qualities

perforce doth move me: forces me

gleek: jest, make a joke

serve mine own turn: for my needs

tend upon: wait on, serve

state: rank

the deep: the ocean

purge thy mortal grossness: get rid of your human
clumsiness

With orange-tawny bill,   120
The throstle with his note so true,
The wren with little quill–

TITANIA   [*Awaking*] What angel wakes me from my
flowery bed?

BOTTOM   [*Sings*]

The finch, the sparrow, and the lark,
The plain-song cuckoo grey,
Whose note full many a man doth mark,
And dares not answer, nay–

for indeed, who would set his wit to so foolish a
bird? Who would give a bird the lie, though he
cry 'cuckoo' never so?   130

TITANIA   I pray thee, gentle mortal, sing again.
Mine ear is much enamoured of thy note;
So is mine eye enthralled to thy shape,
And thy fair virtue's force perforce doth move me,
On the first view to say, to swear, I love thee.

BOTTOM   Methinks mistress, you should have little reason
for that. And yet, to say the truth, reason and
love keep little company together now-a-days.
The more the pity that some honest neighbours
will not make them friends. Nay, I can gleek   140
upon occasion.

TITANIA   Thou art as wise as thou art beautiful.

BOTTOM   Not so neither. But if I had wit enough to get out of
this wood, I have enough to serve mine own turn.

TITANIA   Out of this wood do not desire to go.
Thou shalt remain here, whether thou wilt or no.
I am a spirit of no common rate.
The summer still doth tend upon my state,
And I do love thee; therefore, go with me.
I'll give thee fairies to attend on thee;   150
And they shall fetch thee jewels from the deep,
And sing, while thou on pressed flowers dost sleep.
And I will purge thy mortal grossness so,

**Titania calls on four fairies to wait on Bottom. He
finds something pleasant to say to each of them.**

in his eyes: before him, in his sight
apricocks: apricots
dewberries: berries, a bit like blackberries
for night-tapers ... thighs: collect beeswax for candles
nod: bow your head
courtesies: kindnesses

1 The four fairies greet Bottom and he answers each one
   politely.

That thou shalt like an airy spirit go.
Peaseblossom, Cobweb, Moth, and Mustardseed!

Enter PEASEBLOSSOM, COBWEB, MOTH, *and*
MUSTARDSEED

PEASEBLOSSOM Ready

COBWEB   And I.

MOTH   And I.

MUSTARDSEED   And I.

ALL   Where shall we go?

TITANIA   Be kind and courteous to this gentleman,
                Hop in his walks and gambol in his eyes,
                Feed him with apricocks and dewberries,   159
                With purple grapes, green figs, and mulberries.
                The honey-bags steal from the humble-bees,
                And for night-tapers crop their waxen thighs,
                And light them at the fiery glow-worm's eyes,
                To have my love to bed and to arise;
                And pluck the wings from painted butterflies,
                To fan the moonbeams from his sleeping eyes.
                Nod to him elves, and do him courtesies.

PEASEBLOSSOM Hail, mortal!

COBWEB   Hail!

MOTH   Hail!

MUSTARDSEED   Hail!

BOTTOM   I cry your worships mercy heartily. I beseech
                your worship's name.   170

COBWEB   Cobweb.

BOTTOM   I shall desire you of more acquaintance, good
                Master Cobweb. If I cut my finger, I shall make
                bold with you. Your name honest gentleman?

PEASEBLOSSOM Peaseblossom.

BOTTOM   I pray you commend me to Mistress Squash
                your mother, and to Master Peascod your father.
                Good Master Peaseblossom, I shall desire you of

When Bottom has finished greeting all the fairies Titania tells them to lead him away in silence.

2 Titania orders the fairies to bring Bottom quietly away.

2

Keeping track

1 Why are Bottom, Quince and the others meeting together in the wood?
2 How do they solve the problem of needing the moon to shine during their performance?
3 Who overhears their rehearsal?
4 What prank is played on Bottom and the other workmen, and by whom?
5 Why does Titania fall in love with Bottom?
6 Who is in charge of the rehearsal, Bottom or Quince?
7 Why are the workmen so worried about frightening the ladies?

more acquaintance too. Your name I beseech
you sir?   180

MUSTARDSEED Mustardseed.

BOTTOM   Good Master Mustardseed, I know your
          patience well. That same cowardly, giant-like
          ox-beef hath devoured many a gentleman of
          your house. I promise you your kindred hath
          made my eyes water ere now. I desire you of
          more acquaintance, good Master Mustardseed.

TITANIA   Come wait upon, lead him to my bower.
          The moon methinks looks with a watery eye,
          And when she weeps, weeps every little flower,   190
          Lamenting some enforced chastity.
          Tie up my love's tongue, bring him silently. [*Exeunt*

Drama

...and then she said...

In pairs.
Imagine you are two of the fairies from this scene gossiping
about Titania's behaviour.
1 Decide what gestures you might use.
2 Think about the sort of voices you might have.
3 Role-play the conversation.

Photographs

In fours.
Illustrate the events of the scene in four photographs (see
Photographs, page 197). Select one of these images and
develop it into a two minute scene which is part of either a

Hollywood multi-million pound film or a television soap-opera, such as 'Home and Away'.

Close study

1 What mistakes do the workmen make in their speeches? Make a list of them and then write what they meant to say beside it.

2 What changes in mood and action do you notice in this scene? With a partner, make a chart showing:
   ● the characters involved in each section of the scene
   ● the sequence of events
   ● the mood of each section
   ● the writing style whether it is prose, blank or rhymed verse (see pages 200–202 for help with these).

   Note any conclusions you reach about these.

3 (Lines 8-68) The workmen are concerned with how they will present their play so that it won't offend the audience. They suggest adding a series of prologues to reassure the audience.
   ● What technical problems of staging do they discuss?
   ● How do they decide to solve them?
   ● What other devices does Shakespeare use in this scene to remind us we're watching a play?
   ● What effect would these reminders have on an audience?

Writing

1 Imagine Quince and the other workmen reporting their view of the events of this night to *Athenian Tribune*, their local paper. Write the article a reporter might produce from it.

2 Quince plans to draw up 'a bill of properties' (props, costumes and so on) which will be useful for this play. Make your own list, explaining how each one could be

used in *Pyramus and Thisby*.

3 Imagine the feelings of Quince and the other workmen as they are chased by Puck. Write a description of the events from their point of view.

4 If this were a modern musical, what sort of song would Titania sing to Bottom? Write some lyrics for her.

Quiz

Who said:
1 Are we all met?
2 We will have such a prologue
3 I'll lead you about a round
4 Thou art as wise as thou art beautiful

Complete the following quotations:
5 to say the truth, _____ and love keep little company these days
6 This is to make an _____ of me.

When Oberon and Puck meet up, Puck tells him that Titania is in love with a monster. He starts to describe the workmen's rehearsal, and how he fixed an ass's head on Bottom.

1 Oberon is wondering what creature Titania has been forced to fall in love with.

2 Puck returns and tells him that Titania is in love with a monster.

3 Puck tells Oberon how he created an ass-headed human for Titania to fall in love with. He shows his enjoyment of the trick he has played, as he describes how the other workmen took fright and ran away.

SCENE 2

The wood

Enter OBERON

OBERON   I wonder if Titania be awaked;
Then, what it was the next came in her eye,
Which she must dote on in extremity.

Enter PUCK

Here comes my messenger. How now, mad
    spirit?
What night-rule now about this haunted grove?

PUCK   My mistress with a monster is in love.
Near to her close and consecrated bower,
While she was in her dull and sleeping hour,
A crew of patches, rude mechanicals,
That work for bread upon Athenian stalls,   10
Were met together to rehearse a play
Intended for great Theseus' nuptial day.
The shallowest thick-skin of that barren sort,
Who Pyramus presented, in their sport
Forsook his scene and entered in a brake,
When I did him at this advantage take.
An ass's nole I fixed on his head.
Anon his Thisby must be answered,
And forth my mimic comes. When they him
    spy,
As wild geese that the creeping fowler eye,   20

Puck left Bottom in a place where Titania would wake up and fall in love with him. Oberon is delighted. Puck also claims he has dealt with Demetrius, but when Hermia and Demetrius appear, arguing. Oberon realises Puck has made a mistake.

4 Oberon is very pleased with the story and the fact that Titania is in love with a human ass. He asks whether Puck found the Athenian man he mentioned and Puck says he did and has put the juice in his eyes.

5 When Demetrius and Helena come along Oberon says this is the Athenian he meant. Puck agrees it is the same woman he saw, but not the man he found and treated.

rebuke: scold, reprove
Lay ... foe: call your bitterest enemy such unkind names
Now ... chide: At present I am only scolding
use: treat
o'er shoes: ankle-deep. If he has started by killing Lysander, he should now wallow in blood and kill Hermia too.

4 ⟩

5 ⟩

Or russet-pated choughs, many in sort,
Rising and cawing at the gun's report,
Sever themselves, and madly sweep the sky,
So, at his sight, away his fellows fly;
And, at our stamp, here o'er and o'er one falls;
He 'murder' cries and help from Athens calls.
Their sense thus weak, lost with their fears thus
    strong,
Made senseless things begin to do them wrong.
For briars and thorns at their apparel snatch,
Some sleeves, some hats; from yielders all things
    catch.   30
I led them on in this distracted fear,
And left sweet Pyramus translated there.
When in that moment, so it came to pass,
Titania waked and straightway loved an ass.

OBERON   This falls out better than I could devise.
But hast thou yet latched the Athenian's eyes
With the love-juice, as I did bid thee do?

PUCK   I took him sleeping– that is finished too–
And the Athenian woman by his side;
That when he waked, of force she must be eyed.   40

Enter HERMIA *and* DEMETRIUS

OBERON   Stand close, this is the same Athenian.

PUCK   This is the woman, but not this the man.

DEMETRIUS   O why rebuke you him that loves you so?
Lay breath so bitter on your bitter foe.

HERMIA   Now I but chide, but I should use thee worse,
For thou, I fear, has given me cause to curse.
If thou hast slain Lysander in his sleep,
Being o'er shoes in blood, plunge in the deep,

Hermia thinks that Demetrius must have killed Lysander - otherwise he would never have abandoned her. She goes on accusing Demetrius until he denies it.

as soon: as readily

whole: solid. Hermia's idea is that the moon, creeping through a hole bored right through the centre of the earth will bring night to what would otherwise be daylight (the moon's brother is the sun) on the other side of the world.

dead: deadly

Venus: the name for the goddess of beauty and love.

glimmering: shimmering, glittering

Henceforth ... men: If Demetrius has killed Lysander he has given up the right to be counted as a human being.

Durst ... awake?: Would you have dared to look at him if he was awake?

brave touch!: a fine stroke!

worm: snake

doubler: an adder has a forked (double) tongue, but doubler also means 'more deceitful'

passion: passionate outburst

misprised mood: anger which is mistaken

for aught that: as far as

And kill me too.
The sun was not so true unto the day   50
As he to me. Would he have stolen away
From sleeping Hermia? I'll believe as soon
This whole earth may be bored, and that the
    moon
May through the centre creep, and so displease
Her brother's noontide with th' Antipodes.
It cannot be but thou hast murdered him.
So should a murderer look; so dead, so grim.

DEMETRIUS   So should the murdered look, and so should I,
Pierced through the heart with your stern cruelty.
Yet you, the murderer, look as bright, as clear,   60
As yonder Venus in her glimmering sphere.

HERMIA   What's this to my Lysander? Where is he?
Ah good Demetrius, wilt thou give him me?

DEMETRIUS   I had rather give his carcass to my hounds.

HERMIA   Out dog, out cur! Thou drivest me past the bounds
Of maiden's patience. Hast thou slain him then?
Henceforth be never numbered among men.
O, once tell true; tell true, even for my sake.
Durst thou have looked upon him being awake?
And hast thou killed him sleeping? O brave
    touch.   70
Could not a worm, an adder, do so much?
An adder did it; for with doubler tongue
Than thine, thou serpent, never adder stung.

DEMETRIUS   You spend your passion on a misprised mood.
I am not guilty of Lysander's blood;
Nor is he dead, for aught that I can tell.

HERMIA   I pray thee, tell me then that he is well.

DEMETRIUS   An if I could, what should I get therefore?

HERMIA   A privilege never to see me more.
And from thy hated presence part I so.   80
See me no more, whether he be dead or no.

Demetrius realises there's no point in following her when she is so angry and as he is sad and tired he lies down to sleep. Oberon scolds Puck for treating the wrong man with the juice and sends him to fetch Helena. Meanwhile he treats Demetrius' eyes.
Puck returns, saying that he has brought Helena, with Lysander following her, begging for her love.

---

vein: mood

So sorrow's ... grow: a play on words using 'heavy' to mean 'sad, heavy-hearted' and 'sleepy'

For debt ... sorrow owe: As a result of the sleeplessness caused by sorrow

tender: offer

misprision: misunderstanding, mistake

perforce: inevitably

ensue: result

Then fate ... oath on oath: Fate directs that for every one man who remains true in love, a million more do not, swearing oaths and breaking them again and again.

fancy-sick: love-sick

cheer: face, complexion

sighs of love ... dear: It was believed that each sigh caused the loss of a drop of blood.

against: ready for when

Tartar: Central Asian tribes famous for their fierceness in battle.

apple: pupil

                                                         [Exit

DEMETRIUS   There is no following her in this fierce vein.
               Here therefore for a while I will remain.
               So sorrow's heaviness doth heavier grow
               For debt that bankrupt sleep doth sorrow owe;
               Which now in some slight measure it will pay,
               If for his tender here I make some stay.
                                 [Lies down and sleeps

OBERON   What hast thou done? Thou hast mistaken quite,
               And laid the love-juice on some true-love's sight.
               Of thy misprision must perforce ensue   90
               Some true love turned, and not a false turned true.

PUCK   Then fate o'er-rules, that one man holding troth,
               A million fail, confounding oath on oath.

OBERON   About the wood go swifter than the wind,
               And Helena of Athens look thou find.
               All fancy-sick she is and pale of cheer,
               With sighs of love, that costs the fresh blood dear:
               By some illusion see thou bring her here.
               I'll charm his eyes against she do appear.

PUCK   I go, I go, look how I go,   100
               Swifter than arrow from the Tartar's bow.   *[Exit*

OBERON   Flower of this purple dye,
                        Hit with Cupid's archery,
                        Sink in apple of his eye.

      [He squeezes the flower on Demetrius' eyes

                      When his love he doth espy,
                      Let her shine as gloriously
                      As the Venus of the sky.
                      When thou wakest, if she be by,
                      Beg of her for remedy.

Enter PUCK

PUCK   Captain of our fairy band,   110
                      Helena is here at hand,

Oberon thinks the noise Helena and Lysander are
making will wake Demetrius. Puck is looking forward
to seeing two men wooing one woman. Helena is
protesting that Lysander is only mocking her, when
Demetrius wakes up. He, too, now swears love to
Helena, and praises her beauty.

---

fee: payment

fond pageant: foolish spectacle

alone: unequalled, unique

Look when: whenever

and vows ... appears: vows born in tears must be true

badge of faith: i.e. the tears already referred to

When truth kills truth: the new 'truth' contradicts the
former 'truth' of his love for Hermia. The conflict is
'devilish-holy' because it contains the holiness of truth
and the devilish element that both 'truths' cannot
possibly be true.

fray: conflict, battle

nothing weigh: no weight will register because the scales
will be evenly balanced.

tales: stories, falsehoods

congealed: frozen

Taurus: mountain range in Turkey

princess: paragon, perfection

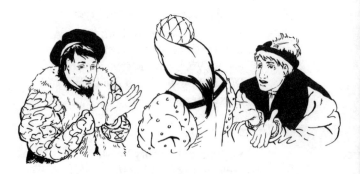

	And the youth, mistook by me,
	Pleading for a lover's fee.
	Shall we their fond pageant see?
	Lord, what fools these mortals be!
OBERON	Stand aside. The noise they make
	Will cause Demetrius to awake.
PUCK	Then will two at once woo one,
	That must needs be sport alone.
	And those things do best please me 120
	That befall preposterously.

Enter LYSANDER *and* HELENA

LYSANDER	Why should you think that I should woo in scorn?
	Scorn and derision never come in tears.
	Look when I vow, I weep; and vows so born,
	In their nativity all truth appears.
	How can these things in me seem scorn to you,
	Bearing the badge of faith to prove them true?
HELENA	You do advance your cunning more and more.
	When truth kills truth, O devilish-holy fray!
	These vows are Hermia's. Will you give her o'er? 130
	Weigh oath with oath, and you will nothing weigh.
	Your vows to her and me, put in two scales,
	Will even weigh, and both as light as tales.
LYSANDER	I had no judgement when to her I swore.
HELENA	Nor none, in my mind, now you give her o'er.
LYSANDER	Demetrius loves her, and he loves not you.
DEMETRIUS	[*Awaking*] O Helen, goddess, nymph, perfect, divine!
	To what, my love, shall I compare thine eyne?
	Crystal is muddy. O, how ripe in show
	Thy lips, those kissing cherries, tempting grow! 140
	That pure congealed white, high Taurus' snow,
	Fanned with the eastern wind, turns to a crow
	When thou hold'st up thy hand. O let me kiss

Helena is angry at her treatment and turns on them
both. They both swear they love only her and Hermia
counts for nothing. Hermia comes in looking for
Lysander.

---

seal: pledge
bent: determined
civil: kind, decent
join in souls: team up
parts: qualities
trim: fine
sort: rank
extort: torture
you sport: fun, amusement for yourselves
I will none: I don't want anything to do with her
but ... sojourned: visited her as a guest
aby it dear: pay dearly for it
his: its
Dark night ... makes: The darkness of night, which robs
    the eye of its power to see, makes the ear more sensitive.

This princess of pure white, this seal of bliss.

HELENA   O spite! O hell! I see you all are bent
To set against me for your merriment.
If you were civil and knew courtesy,
You would not do me thus much injury.
Can you not hate me, as I know you do,
But you must join in souls to mock me too?   150
If you were men, as men you are in show,
You would not use a gentle lady so;
To vow, and swear, and superpraise my parts,
When I am sure you hate me with your hearts.
You both are rivals, and love Hermia;
And now both rivals, to mock Helena.
A trim exploit, a manly enterprise,
To conjure tears up in a poor maid's eyes
With your derision. None of noble sort
Would so offend a virgin, and extort   160
A poor soul's patience, all to make you sport.

LYSANDER   You are unkind, Demetrius; be not so,
For you love Hermia; this you know I know.
And here, with all good will, with all my heart,
In Hermia's love I yield you up my part;
And yours of Helena to me bequeath,
Whom I do love, and will do till my death.

HELENA   Never did mockers waste more idle breath.

DEMETRIUS   Lysander, keep thy Hermia; I will none.
If e'er I loved her, all that love is gone.   170
My heart to her but as guest-wise sojourned,
And now to Helen is it home returned,
There to remain.

LYSANDER   Helen, it is not so.

DEMETRIUS   Disparage not the faith thou dost not know,
Lest to thy peril thou aby it dear.
Look where thy love comes; yonder is thy dear.

Enter HERMIA

HERMIA   Dark night, that from the eye his function takes,

Hermia now learns that Lysander hates her. Her amazement makes Helena think that all three of them have teamed up to make fun of her. She appeals to Hermia to remember what friends they used to be.

Wherein ... recompense: Although it causes our sight to fail, it makes our hearing twice as sharp to compensate for this.

bide: stay

engilds: makes shine

yon fiery ... light: stars. An 'o' was both an orb, and a silver spangle.

confederacy: conspiracy, plot

conjoined: joined together, united

fashion: create, make

sport: entertainment

in spite of me: to spite me, to annoy me

bait: tease, torment

derision: mockery

counsel: confidences

chid ... parting us: scolded time for passing so quickly that it was time to part

artificial: skilful at making things, creative

sampler: a piece of embroidery

incorporate: belonging to one body

an union in partition: a single person in two bodies

	The ear more quick of apprehension makes.	
	Wherein it doth impair the seeing sense,	
	It pays the hearing double recompense.	180
	Thou art not by mine eye, Lysander, found;	
	Mine ear, I thank it, brought me to thy sound.	
	But why unkindly didst thou leave me so?	
LYSANDER	Why should he stay, whom love doth press to go?	
HERMIA	What love could press Lysander from my side?	
LYSANDER	Lysander's love, that would not let him bide,	
	Fair Helena, who more engilds the night	
	Than all yon fiery oes and eyes of light.	
	Why seek'st thou me? Could not this make thee know,	
	The hate I bear thee made me leave thee so?	190
HERMIA	You speak not as you think; it cannot be.	
HELENA	Lo, she is one of this confederacy.	
	Now I perceive they have conjoined all three	
	To fashion this false sport in spite of me.	
	Injurious Hermia, most ungrateful maid,	
	Have you conspired, have you with these contrived	
	To bait me with this foul derision?	
	Is all the counsel that we two have shared,	
	The sisters' vows, the hours that we have spent,	
	When we have chid the hasty-footed time	200
	For parting us–O, is all forgot?	
	All school-days' friendship, childhood innocence?	
	We, Hermia, like two artificial gods,	
	Have with our needles created both one flower,	
	Both on one sampler, sitting on one cushion,	
	Both warbling of one song, both in one key,	
	As if our hands, our sides, voices, and minds	
	Had been incorporate. So we grew together,	
	Like to a double cherry, seeming parted,	
	But yet an union in partition,	210
	Two lovely berries moulded on one stem.	
	So with two seeming bodies, but one heart,	

Hermia is completely at a loss to understand what is happening. Helena thinks it's all a cruel plot to have a good joke at her expense. She decides to leave. Lysander begs her to stay.

Two of the first … crest: an image from heraldry. 'The first' refers back to 'bodies'. A shield, used as a coat of arms, may have two or four divisions - halves or quarters - and while the same device may appear twice, the whole design appears under one crest and belongs to one person.

rent asunder: tear apart

chide: scold

even but now: just now, a moment ago

spurn … foot: kick me aside

forsooth: indeed

But … setting on: except through your encouragement

grace: favour

hung upon: loaded down with

miserable most: the most miserable of women

Persever: carry on

counterfeit: put on falsely

make mouths upon me: pull faces at me

hold the sweet jest up: carry on with your charming little joke

chronicled: written about

argument: object of cruel joking

1 Hermia asks Lysander not to scorn Helena in this way.

1

	Two of the first, like coats in heraldry,
	Due but to one, and crowned with one crest.
	And will you rent our ancient love asunder,
	To join with men in scorning your poor friend?
	It is not friendly, 't is not maidenly.
	Our sex, as well as I, may chide you for it,
	Though I alone do feel the injury.

HERMIA   I am amazed at your passionate words.   220
          I scorn you not. It seems that you scorn me.

HELENA   Have you not set Lysander, as in scorn,
          To follow me and praise my eyes and face?
          And made your other love, Demetrius,
          Who even but now did spurn me with his foot,
          To call me goddess, nymph, divine, and rare,
          Precious, celestial? Wherefore speaks he this
          To her he hates? And wherefore doth Lysander
          Deny your love, so rich within his soul,
          And tender me, forsooth, affection,   230
          But by your setting on, by your consent?
          What though I be not so in grace as you,
          So hung upon with love, so fortunate,
          But miserable most, to love unloved?
          This you should pity rather than despise.

HERMIA   I understand not what you mean by this.

HELENA   Ay, do, persever, counterfeit sad looks.
          Make mouths upon me when I turn my back.
          Wink each at other, hold the sweet jest up.
          This sport well carried, shall be chronicled.   240
          If you have any pity, grace, or manners,
          You would not make me such an argument.
          But fare ye well, 't is partly my own fault,
          Which death or absence soon shall remedy.

LYSANDER Stay gentle Helena, hear my excuse;
          My love, my life, my soul, fair Helena.

HELENA   O excellent!

HERMIA   Sweet, do not scorn her so.

To prove his love for Helena, Lysander challenges Demetrius to a duel. Hermia hangs on Lysander's arm to try to stop him going. Lysander tries to shake her loose, saying that he hates her, but won't harm her. Hermia says hate is the worst harm he can do her, that nothing has really changed.

2 Demetrius says he can force Lysander not to scorn Helena. Lysander says neither of them can have any effect on him, and continues to swear love for Helena. Demetrius does the same.

3 Lysander challenges him to a duel to decide the matter and Demetrius agrees.

4 Hermia hangs on to Lysander, who tries to shake her off, denies her love and calls her names.

5 Lysander assures Demetrius he will fight the duel, although Hermia is trying to prevent him. He says he won't harm Hermia physically to get rid of her, although he hates her.

6 Hermia is completely bewildered at his change of heart and says hate is the greatest harm he can do to her. She tries to persuade him that nothing has changed during the night.

DEMETRIUS   If she cannot entreat, I can compel.

LYSANDER   Thou canst compel no more than she entreat.
            Thy threats have no more strength than her
                weak prayers.   250
            Helen, I love thee, by my life I do.
            I swear by that which I will lose for thee,
            To prove him false that says I love thee not.

DEMETRIUS   I say I love thee more than he can do.

LYSANDER   If thou say so, withdraw, and prove it too.

DEMETRIUS   Quick, come–

HERMIA   Lysander, whereto tends all this?

LYSANDER   Away, you Ethiop!

DEMETRIUS   No, no; he'll
            Seem to break loose. Take on as you would follow,
            But yet come not. You are a tame man, go!

LYSANDER   Hang off thou cat, thou burr! Vile thing let loose,
            Or I will shake thee from me like a serpent.   261

HERMIA   Why are you grown so rude? What change is this,
            Sweet love?

LYSANDER   Thy love? Out tawny Tartar, out!
            Out, loathed medicine! O hated potion, hence!

HERMIA   Do you not jest?

HELENA   Yes sooth, and so do you.

LYSANDER   Demetrius, I will keep my word with thee.

DEMETRIUS   I would I had your bond, for I perceive
            A weak bond holds you. I'll not trust your word.

LYSANDER   What, should I hurt her, strike her, kill her dead?
            Although I hate her, I'll not harm her so.   270

HERMIA   What, can you do me greater harm than hate?
            Hate me, wherefore? O me, what news, my love?
            Am not I Hermia? Are not you Lysander?
            I am as fair now as I was erewhile.
            Since night you loved me; yet since night you left
                me.

**When, in spite of this appeal, Lysander assures her
that he wants her out of his sight for ever, that there
is no hope for her, and that he hates her and loves
Helena, Hermia turns on her former friend.**

7 Lysander tells Hermia that she must be absolutely
certain that he hates her and loves Helena.

7 >

juggler: trickster
canker-blossom: grub that destroys flower buds and
leaves
Fine, i' faith: Helena is sarcastic; she still thinks that
Hermia has joined the men in making fun of her
counterfeit: fraud
puppet: there are many references to Hermia's shortness.
statures: heights
She hath urged her height: she's used her height to gain
an advantage
prevailed: succeeded
painted: Hermia says Helena has used make-up to
improve her complexion
maypole: the tall pole which people danced around on
May 1st. The emphasis is again on Helena's height.
curst: bad-tempered
shrewishness: quarrelling and insulting people

Why then you left me–O, the gods forbid–
In earnest, shall I say?

LYSANDER   Ay, by my life.
And never did desire to see thee more.
Therefore be out of hope, of question, of doubt.
Be certain, nothing truer; 't is no jest   280
That I do hate thee and love Helena.

HERMIA   O me, you juggler, you canker-blossom,
You thief of love. What, have you come by night
And stolen my love's heart from him?

HELENA   Fine, i' faith!
Have you no modesty, no maiden shame,
No touch of bashfulness? What, will you tear
Impatient answers from my gentle tongue?
Fie, fie, you counterfeit, you puppet, you!

HERMIA   Puppet? Why so? Ay, that way goes the game.
Now I perceive that she hath made compare   290
Between our statures, she hath urged her height,
And with her personage, her tall personage,
Her height, forsooth, she hath prevailed with him.
And are you grown so high in his esteem,
Because I am so dwarfish and so low?
How low am I, thou painted maypole? Speak;
How low am I? I am not yet so low,
But that my nails can reach unto thine eyes.

HELENA   I pray you, though you mock me, gentlemen,
Let her not hurt me. I was never curst.   300
I have no gift at all in shrewishness.
I am a right maid for my cowardice.
Let her not strike me. You perhaps may think,
Because she is something lower than myself.
That I can match her.

HERMIA   Lower? Hark, again.

HELENA   Good Hermia, do not be so bitter with me.
I evermore did love you Hermia,
Did ever keep your counsels, never wronged you;

Helena sadly offers to leave, but the quarrel flares up
again and this time the men can scarcely keep
Hermia and Helena apart. The two men leave to fight
their duel.

---

chid me hence: told me to go away
so: if
folly: foolish behaviour
fond: foolish
keen: bitter
shrewd: sharp
suffer her to flout me this: allow her to insult me like this
minimus: tiny creature
knot grass: low-growing grass. The juice of it was given to
dwarves kept as court entertainers, to stunt their growth.
officious: eager to do your duty
for if ... aby it: for if you show even the slightest amount
of affection for her, you will be made to pay for it.
cheek by jowl: side by side

Save that, in love unto Demetrius,
I told him of your stealth unto this wood.   310
He followed you; for love I followed him.
But he hath chid me hence and threatened me
To strike me, spurn me; nay, to kill me too.
And now, so you will let me quiet go,
To Athens will I bear my folly back,
And follow you no further. Let me go.
You see how simple and how fond I am.

HERMIA   Why, get you gone. Who is 't that hinders you?

HELENA   A foolish heart, that I leave here behind.

HERMIA   What with Lysander?

HELENA   With Demetrius.   320

LYSANDER   Be not afraid; she shall not harm thee Helena.

DEMETRIUS No sir, she shall not, though you take her part.

HELENA   O, when she's angry, she is keen and shrewd.
She was a vixen when she went to school;
And though she be but little, she is fierce.

HERMIA   'Little' again? Nothing but 'low' and 'little'.
Why will you suffer her to flout me thus?
Let me come to her.

LYSANDER   Get you gone, you dwarf,
You minimus, of hindering knot-grass made,
You bead, you acorn.

DEMETRIUS   You are too officious   330
In her behalf that scorns your services.
Let her alone; speak not of Helena;
Take not her part. For, if thou dost intend
Never so little show of love to her,
Thou shalt aby it.

LYSANDER   Now she holds me not.
Now follow, if thou dar'est, to try whose right,
Of thine or mine, is most in Helena.

DEMETRIUS Follow? Nay, I'll go with thee, cheek by jowl.
                              [*Exeunt Lysander and Demetrius*

Afraid of a fight with Hermia, Helena runs off.
Hermia leaves too. Oberon tells Puck off for making
such a bad mistake and orders him to use magic to
keep Lysander and Demetrius from fighting.

coil: fuss, bother
'long of you: on account of you
curst: quarrelsome, bad-tempered
fray: fight

1 Oberon and Puck appear when all the humans have
  gone and Oberon is cross with Puck for treating
  Lysander with juice instead of Demetrius. He has
  made a lot of mistakes recently - or he's doing it on
  purpose.
2 Oberon tells Puck to create a magic fog and to imitate
  their voices so that Lysander and Demetrius will be
  led astray and will be unable to fight the intended
  duel.
3 When they fall asleep, exhausted, Puck is to crush a
  second herb into Lysander's eye, so that he can see
  normally. The lovers will then go back to Athens and
  live happily ever after.

HERMIA   You, mistress, all this coil is 'long of you.
          Nay, go not back.

HELENA   I will not trust you, I,   340
          Nor longer stay in your curst company.
          Your hands than mine are quicker for a fray,
          My legs are longer though, to run away.   [*Exit*

HERMIA   I am amazed, and know not what to say.   [*Exit*

OBERON   This is thy negligence. Still thou mistak'st,
          Or else committ'st thy knaveries wilfully.

PUCK   Believe me, king of shadows, I mistook.
          Did not you tell me I should know the man
          By the Athenian garments he had on?
          And so far blameless proves my enterprise,   350
          That I have 'nointed an Athenian's eyes;
          And so far am I glad it so did sort,
          As this their jangling I esteem a sport.

OBERON   Thou see'st these lovers seek a place to fight:
          Hie therefore Robin, overcast the night,
          The starry welkin cover thou anon
          With drooping fog as black as Acheron,
          And lead these testy rivals so astray,
          As one come not within another's way.
          Like to Lysander sometime frame thy tongue, 360
          Then stir Demetrius up with bitter wrong;
          And sometime rail thou like Demetrius;
          And from each other look thou lead them thus,
          Till o'er their brows death-counterfeiting sleep
          With leaden legs and batty wings doth creep.
          Then crush this herb into Lysander's eye,
          Whose liquor hath this virtuous property,
          To take from thence all error with his might,
          And make his eyeballs roll with wonted sight.
          When they next wake, all this derision   370
          Shall seem a dream and fruitless vision,
          And back to Athens shall the lovers wend,
          With league whose date till death shall never end.

Oberon declares that, while Puck is correcting his mistake, he will go and claim the Indian boy he wants from Titania. They will do this as quickly as possible because it will soon be dawn. The two men return and Puck starts to lead them away from one another.

4

5

4 Meanwhile, Oberon will persuade Titania to give him the Indian boy and he will remove the charm from her eyes and all shall be well.

5 Puck suggests they should hurry as it is nearly dawn, when ghosts and spirits must disappear. Oberon says they are different kinds of spirits and need not fear dawn, but that all this can still be achieved before daylight.

6 Puck imitates Demetrius, pretending to find a more suitable place to fight.

6

Whiles I in this affair do thee employ,
I'll to my queen and beg her Indian boy:
And then I will her charmed eye release
From monster's view, and all things shall be peace.

PUCK   My fairy lord, this must be done with haste.
For night's swift dragons cut the clouds full fast,
And yonder shines Aurora's harbinger;   380
At whose approach, ghosts, wandering here and
       there,
Troop home to churchyards; damned spirits all,
That in crossways and floods have burial,
Already to their wormy beds are gone;
For fear lest day should look their shames upon,
They wilfully themselves exile from light,
And must for aye consort with black-browed night.

OBERON   But we are spirits of another sort.
I with the morning's love have oft made sport,
And like a forester the groves may tread,   390
Even till the eastern gate, all fiery-red,
Opening on Neptune with fair blessed beams,
Turns into yellow gold his salt green streams.
But, notwithstanding, haste, make no delay:
We may effect this business yet ere day.   [*Exit*

PUCK   Up and down, up and down,
              I will lead them up and down
              I am feared in field and town.
              Goblin, lead them up and down.
              Here comes one.   400

Enter LYSANDER

LYSANDER   Where art thou, proud Demetrius? Speak thou now.
PUCK   Here villain, drawn and ready. Where art thou?
LYSANDER   I will be with thee straight.
PUCK   Follow me then
       To plainer ground. [*Exit Lysander following the voice*

Puck leads Lysander and Demetrius all over the place, until they separately lie down to sleep. Then Demetrius decides to wait until daylight to find and fight his enemy.

7 Puck uses Lysander's voice to taunt Demetrius.
8 Lysander quickly gets tired and exasperated and decides to give up the idea of a duel until daylight.
9 Demetrius is soon expressing the same feelings. Puck has successfully carried out Oberon's instructions.

7 >

8 >

9 >

Enter DEMETRIUS

DEMETRIUS   Lysander, speak again.
Thou runaway, thou coward, art thou fled?
Speak! In some bush? Where dost thou hide thy
     head?

PUCK   Thou coward, art thou bragging to the stars,
Telling the bushes that thou look'st for wars.
And wilt not come? Come recreant, come thou
     child,
I'll whip thee with a rod. He is defiled   410
That draws a sword on thee.

DEMETRIUS   Yea, art thou there?

PUCK   Follow my voice; we'll try no manhood here.
                                        [*Exeunt*

Enter LYSANDER

LYSANDER   He goes before me and still dares me on.
When I come where he calls, then he is gone.
The villain is much lighter-heeled than I,
I followed fast, but faster he did fly;
That fallen am I in dark uneven way,
And here will rest me. [*Lies down.*] Come thou
     gentle day,
For if but once thou show me thy grey light,
I'll find Demetrius and revenge this spite. [*Sleeps*

Enter PUCK *and* DEMETRIUS

PUCK   Ho, ho, ho! Coward, why comest thou not? 421

DEMETRIUS   Abide me if thou darest, for well I wot
Thou runn'st before me, shifting every place,
And darest not stand, nor look me in the face.
Where art thou now?

PUCK   Come hither; I am here.

DEMETRIUS   Nay then thou mock'st me. Thou shalt buy this
     dear,
If ever I thy face by daylight see.

Helena comes to the same place, not seeing the men in the darkness and lies down to sleep. Shortly afterwards Hermia comes along, exhausted, and goes to sleep, hoping that Lysander will come to no harm. Puck puts the juice on Lysander's eyes, so that he will fall in love again with the woman he really loves.

10 ⟩

10   Helena comes along, tired and sad, and waiting for
     the dawn, so that she can go back to Athens in
     daylight. She too lies down and falls asleep.

knavish: wicked
bedabbled: sprinkled
My legs ... desires: my legs won't obey me any more
Heavens shield ... fray: May Heaven protect Lysander if
   they (Lysander and Demetrius) intend to fight

Now, go thy way. Faintness constraineth me
To measure out my length on this cold bed.
By day's approach look to be visited.   430

[Lies down and sleeps

Enter HELENA

HELENA O weary night, O long and tedious night,
Abate thy hours. Shine comforts from the east,
That I may back to Athens by daylight,
From these that my poor company detest.
And sleep, that sometimes shuts up sorrow's eye,
Steal me awhile from mine own company.

[Lies down and sleeps

PUCK   Yet but three? Come one more.
Two of both kinds makes up four.
Here she comes, curst and sad.
Cupid is a knavish lad,   440
Thus to make poor females mad.

Enter HERMIA

HERMIA Never so weary, never so in woe,
Bedabbled with the dew, and torn with briers,
I can no further crawl, no further go;
My legs can keep no pace with my desires.
Here will I rest me till the break of day.
Heavens shield Lysander, if they mean a fray.

[Lies down and sleeps

PUCK   On the ground
Sleep sound;
I'll apply   450
To your eye
Gentle lover, remedy.

[Puts the juice on Lysander's eyes

When thou wak'st,
Thou tak'st
True delight
In the sight

Puck says that everything will be all right.

Jack shall have Jill: the man shall have his girl
The man shall have his mare again: Puck uses proverbs to
 tell us that all will end happily.

ACTIVITIES

Keeping track

1 When Puck says 'My mistress with a monster is in love'
   (line 6), what is he talking about?
2 Oberon chastises Puck with 'What hast thou done?' (line
   88) What has he done?
3 Why does Lysander say this and to whom is it said?
   'Why should you think that I should woo in scorn?' (line
   122)
4 Why does Helena make this statement and for whom is it
   intended?
   'You do advance your cunning more and more.' (line 128)

Discussion

1 The love of Helena, Hermia, Lysander and Demetrius
   becomes entangled and confused, thanks to the meddling of
   Oberon and Puck. Why and how did they become involved?
2 The world of Oberon and Titania has been described as
   'the fairy world' by some. Find examples in this scene
   which would suggest that this is really quite a good label.
   Can you think of a more appropriate name? Consider the
   reasons for your choice.

Of thy former lady's eye.
And the country proverb known,
That every man should take his own,
In your waking shall be shown.   460
Jack shall have Jill;
Nought shall go ill;
The man shall have his mare again, and all
shall be well.

[*Exit*

3 Can you find any evidence which suggests that Helena and
   Hermia are represented as stereotypes of women in love?
   Are the men stereotypes in their behaviour and attitude?
   What might be the reasons for this?

Drama

In a small group.

1 How do you think a director could present the taunting of
   Lysander and Demetrius by Puck?
   ● Read this section of the play carefully
   ● Discuss how it should be presented.
   ● Make a list of the main actions.
   ● Prepare a script. Use Shakespeare's text and add your
     own stage directions, prop lists, sound effects etc.
2 Now try the same thing again, but using everyday
   language.
3 Helena and Hermia decide to look for more suitable
   partners. They try out a video dating service. Write their
   scripts and enact the result.

Character

1 Puck says 'As this their jangling I esteem a sport' (line 353), to indicate that he is thoroughly enjoying the confusion of the lovers. Find other examples in the scene which show Puck enjoying being a nuisance. What is your opinion of him?

2 'Oberon is a dominant character'. What evidence can you find that agrees with this statement?

3 Helena and Hermia are supposed to be good friends. They say many hurtful things to each other in this scene. Find examples of these and explain why each of the characters would be dismayed by what the other said.

4 Add to your Character logs for Oberon, Puck and the lovers.

Close study

1 Identify the spells and chants that Puck uses in this scene. Look closely at lines 448 to 463, follow the pattern of rhythm and rhyme and make up a spell of your own.

2 Lysander and Demetrius are extravagant in their adoration of Helena, (lines 137-144, 187-188) and uncomplimentary to Hermia, (lines 260-61, 277-81).
   ● Make a list of the words that are used
   ● Think about how you could present these ideas visually as a poster. You could use pictures of the four characters, arrows, colours - anything that gets the ideas across.

Writing

1 Prepare a detailed letter of complaint to the local *Woodland Bugle*, as written by the Badger family. They have recently endured a very unsettling evening in their part of the woods, due to all of the 'goings on

above ground', thanks to the somewhat unwelcome two-legged visitors.

2 Write Puck's job description, detailing his role, duties, etc. Make a list of anything he is not allowed to do and any other important points about his 'job'.

3 Write a letter from Puck to the Personnel Manager of Sprite Assistants Inc., complaining of the raw deal which he is having whilst with his present master. Remember, he is likely to refer to previous, more 'attractive' overlords.

4 Choose one of the four lovers. Write in role as that person about your feelings concerning your situation at this point in the story. Choose one of these formats:
- diary
- letter to a friend
- letter to your solicitor, business manager, or agent
- letter to Duke Theseus
- a 'true confession' that you are planning to bury deep underground somewhere in the forest.

5 Trust is an important element in any sound relationship. Describe what has happened to the trust in the relationships which were portrayed in this scene.

Quiz

1 Fill in the missing words.

_____ places love juice in the eyes of_____ .

He now hates _____ and loves _____ .

_____ also loves _____ .

In conclusion, in this scene _____ is courted by _____ and _____ .

_____ feels like a spare part.

2 Identify quotations which support both sides of the arguments for these statements:
- Helena does not trust Hermia ....
- Hermia does not trust Helena ....

3 What do you think might happen next?

The four lovers are lying asleep while Oberon, also unseen, watches Titania sitting with Bottom, while her fairies wait on him.

1 Titania is in love with Bottom, complete with his ass's head. She sits with him, stroking his cheek and kissing his ears. Her fairies are there to carry out his orders and Oberon, unseen by them, watches what is going on.

1

Act four

The wood
LYSANDER, DEMETRIUS, HELENA, *and* HERMIA *lying asleep*

Enter TITANIA *and* BOTTOM; PEASEBLOSSOM,
COBWEB, MOTH, MUSTARDSEED, *and other Fairies
attending;* OBERON *behind unseen.*

TITANIA	Come sit thee down upon this flowery bed,
	While I thy amiable cheeks do coy,
	And stick musk-roses in thy sleek smooth head,
	And kiss thy fair large ears, my gentle joy.
BOTTOM	Where's Peaseblossom?
PEASEBLOSSOM	Ready.
BOTTOM	Scratch my head, Peaseblossom. Where's Monsieur Cobweb?
COBWEB	Ready. 9
BOTTOM	Monsieur Cobweb, good monsieur, get you your weapons in your hand, and kill me a red-hipped humble-bee on the top of a thistle; and good monsieur, bring me the honey-bag. Do not fret yourself too much in the action, monsieur; and good monsieur, have a care the honey-bag break not, I would be loth to have you overflown with a honey-bag signior. Where's Monsieur Mustardseed?
MUSTARDSEED	Ready.
BOTTOM	Give me your neaf, Monsieur Mustardseed. Pray you, leave your courtesy, good monsieur. 20
MUSTARDSEED	What's your will?
BOTTOM	Nothing good monsieur, but to help Cavalery Cobweb to scratch. I must to the barber's,

Bottom, offered music, only wants the kind he is used to; offered food he asks for the food a donkey would enjoy. He falls asleep in Titania's arms. Oberon tells Puck he is beginning to feel sorry for Titania, and tells him of his recent meeting with her.

2 Bottom, in this romantic setting, asks for a good scratch; the music he wants is played on the tongs and the bones, very basic instruments; the food he longs for is oats and hay, or dried peas. He soon feels tired and they sleep.

3 Oberon, seeing this grossness, begins to pity her. He tells Puck he has met Titania with Bottom behind the wood. He picked a quarrel with her because she had put a garland of flowers round the ass's head.

	monsieur, for methinks I am marvellous hairy
	about the face. And I am such a tender ass if my
	hair do but tickle me, I must scratch.
TITANIA	What, wilt thou hear some music, my sweet love?
BOTTOM	I have a reasonable good ear in music. Let's have
	the tongs and the bones.
TITANIA	Or say, sweet love, what thou desirest to eat. 30
BOTTOM	Truly a peck of provender. I could munch your
	good dry oats. Methinks I have a great desire to
	a bottle of hay. Good hay, sweet hay, hath no
	fellow.
TITANIA	I have a venturous fairy that shall seek
	The squirrel's hoard, and fetch thee new nuts.
BOTTOM	I had rather have a handful or two of dried peas.
	But, I pray you, let none of your people stir me. I
	have an exposition of sleep come upon me.
TITANIA	Sleep thou, and I will wind thee in my arms. 40
	Fairies be gone, and be all ways away.

[Exeunt fairies

So doth the woodbine, the sweet honeysuckle,
Gently entwist; the female ivy so
Enrings the barky fingers of the elm.
O how I love thee! How I dote on thee!   *[They sleep*

Enter PUCK

OBERON	*[Advancing]* Welcome, good Robin. See'st thou
	this sweet sight?
	Her dotage now I do begin to pity.
	For meeting her of late behind the wood,
	Seeking sweet favours for this hateful fool,
	I did upbraid her and fall out with her. 50
	For she his hairy temples then had rounded
	With coronet of fresh and fragrant flowers.
	And that same dew, which sometime on the buds
	Was wont to swell like round and orient pearls,
	Stood now within the pretty flowerets' eyes

**Oberon was cross with her when he met her with
Bottom. She begged his forgiveness and gave up the
Indian child to him.**

4 ⟩

**Oberon tells Puck to take the ass's head off Bottom's
head, so that all the humans can go back to Athens.
He takes the magic spell off Titania. She wakes up,
hating the sight of Bottom. Puck takes off the ass's
head. Oberon and Titania are together again.**

5 ⟩

4 Oberon teased and taunted her and she then made her
   peace with him and when he asked again for the little
   Indian boy, she gave him up.

5 Now that Oberon has the child, he will take the charm
   away from her eyes. He tells Puck to remove the ass's
   head from Bottom so that everyone can go back to
   Athens thinking that all the night's events have merely
   been a dream.

6 When Titania can see normally again, she hates the
   sight of Bottom. Oberon makes sure that all the
   humans are in a magically deep sleep whilst Puck
   removes the ass's head.

7 Oberon and Titania are reconciled.

6 ⟩

7 ⟩

Like tears that did their own disgrace bewail.
When I had at my pleasure taunted her,
And she in mild terms begged my patience,
I then did ask of her her changeling child,
Which straight she gave me, and her fairy sent   60
To bear him to my bower in Fairyland.
And now I have the boy, I will undo
This hateful imperfection of her eyes.
And, gentle Puck, take this transformed scalp
From off the head of this Athenian swain;
That he, awaking when the other do,
May all to Athens back again repair,
And think no more of this night's accidents,
But as the fierce vexation of a dream.
But first I will release the Fairy Queen.   70
  Be as thou wast wont to be;
  See as thou wast wont to see.
  Dian's bud o'er Cupid's flower
  Hath such force and blessed power.
Now my Titania, wake you, my sweet queen.

TITANIA My Oberon, what visions have I seen!
Methought I was enamoured of an ass.

OBERON There lies your love.

TITANIA   How came these things to pass?
O, how mine eyes do loathe his visage now.

OBERON Silence awhile. Robin, take off this head.   80
Titania, music call, and strike more dead
Than common sleep of all these five the sense.

TITANIA Music, ho! music, such as charmeth sleep.
            [Music

PUCK Now, when thou wak'st, with thine own fool's
  eyes peep.

OBERON Sound, music. Come my queen, take hands with
  me,
And rock the ground whereon these sleepers be.
Now thou and I are new in amity,

Oberon and Titania dance together and promise they will dance in Duke Theseus' palace and bless it. Puck says it will soon be dawn.
They leave and Theseus, Hippolyta, Egeus and their attendants come in. They intend to hunt, and talk about hounds they have seen and heard.

8

9

8 Oberon and Titania dance and promise that after the three weddings they will dance in Duke Theseus' house and bless it.

9 Puck can hear the lark; it will soon be day. As they leave, Titania asks Oberon to explain why she was sleeping so close to four mortals.

find out: look for
observation: celebration of midsummer day
since … day: as it is still early in the day
uncouple: let the hounds go (they have been chained in pairs)
Dispatch: hurry!
mark: listen to
in conjunction: together
Hercules and Cadmus: two heroes of Greek mythology
bayed the bear: hunted the bear until it was cornered and forced to turn and fight the hounds 'at bay'
chiding: (here) barking angrily

	And will tomorrow midnight solemnly
	Dance in Duke Theseus' house triumphantly
	And bless it to all fair prosperity.

And will tomorrow midnight solemnly
Dance in Duke Theseus' house triumphantly
And bless it to all fair prosperity.   90
There shall the pairs of faithful lovers be
Wedded, with Theseus, all in jollity.

PUCK   Fairy King, attend, and mark,
        I do hear the morning lark.

OBERON   Then, my queen, in silence sad,
        Trip we after night's shade.
        We the globe can compass soon,
        Swifter than the wandering moon.

TITANIA   Come my lord, and in our flight,
        Tell me how it came this night   100
        That I sleeping here was found
        With these mortals on the ground. [*Exeunt*
                        [*Wind horns*

Enter THESEUS, HIPPOLYTA, EGEUS, *and* TRAIN

THESEUS   Go one of you, find out the forester;
For now our observation is performed,
And since we have the vaward of the day,
My love shall hear the music of my hounds.
Uncouple in the western valley, let them go.
Dispatch I say, and find the forester.   [*Exit an*
                                  attendant
We will, fair queen, up to the mountain's top,
And mark the musical confusion   110
Of hounds and echo in conjunction.

HIPPOLYTA   I was with Hercules and Cadmus once,
When in a wood of Crete they bayed the bear
With hounds of Sparta; never did I hear
Such gallant chiding. For, besides the groves,
The skies, the fountains, every region near
Seemed all one mutual cry. I never heard
So musical a discord, such sweet thunder.

THESEUS   My hounds are bred out of the Spartan kind,

The talk of hounds continues until Theseus notices
the lovers asleep. Egeus is surprised to see them.
Theseus remembers that this is the day Hermia had
to give her choice: Demetrius or the convent. The
huntsman wakes them with the horn, and, still
drowsy with sleep, Lysander tries to answer their
questions.

---

so flewed: with the same, loose-hanging skin around their
jaws

so sanded: with similar sandy markings

Crook-kneed: with bent legs

dewlapped: with folds of skin around their throats

matched in mouth: chosen for the harmonious sound of
their baying

each under each: some high, some lower in pitch

horn: hunting horn

halloo: the call of the huntsman in the chase

I wonder of: I am surprised at

rite of May: the Mayday/Midsummer celebrations already
referred to (Act 4 scene 1 line 104 and Act 1 scene 1
line 167)

soft: wait a moment, stop

in grace of our solemnity: in honour of our celebrations

Saint Valentine ... now?: Saint Valentine is the patron
saint of lovers and on Saint Valentine's day the birds
were thought to choose their mates.

couple: pair up

jealousy: suspicion

by hate: beside a person who hates you

amazedly: in confusion

do bethink me: come to think about it

	So flewed, so sanded, and their heads are hung 120
	With ears that sweep away the morning dew,
	Crook-kneed, and dew-lapped like Thessalian bulls;
	Slow in pursuit, but matched in mouth like bells,
	Each under each. A cry more tuneable
	Was never hollaed to, nor cheered with horn,
	In Crete, in Sparta, nor in Thessaly.
	Judge when you hear. But soft, what nymphs are these?

EGEUS My lord, this is my daughter here asleep,
And this, Lysander, this Demetrius is,
This Helena, old Nedar's Helena. 130
I wonder of their being here together.

THESEUS No doubt they rose up early to observe
The rite of May; and hearing our intent,
Came here in grace of our solemnity.
But speak, Egeus, is not this the day
That Hermia should give answer of her choice?

EGEUS It is, my lord.

THESEUS Go bid the huntsmen wake them with their horns.
　　　　　[*Wind horns. Shout within. They all start up*
Good morrow, friends. Saint Valentine is past.
Begin these wood-birds but to couple now? 140

LYSANDER Pardon, my lord.

THESEUS 　　　　　　　I pray you all, stand up.
I know you two are rival enemies.
How comes this gentle concord in the world,
That hatred is so far from jealousy,
To sleep by hate, and fear no enmity?

LYSANDER My lord, I shall reply amazedly,
Half sleep, half waking. But as yet, I swear,
I cannot truly say how I came here.
But as I think–for truly would I speak,
And now I do bethink me, so it is– 150
I came with Hermia hither. Our intent
Was to be gone from Athens, where we might

The minute Lysander mentions 'Athenian law' Egeus breaks in, demanding the law deal with him, for taking his daughter away. Demetrius steps in, explaining that Helena now has his love again, and promising it will be for ever. Theseus overrules Egeus and promises a triple wedding.

stealth: stealing away secretly
purpose hither: intention to come here
in fancy: because of love
I wot not: I do not know
remembrance of an idle gaud: memory of a useless toy
I did dote upon: I was foolishly fond of
And all the faith ... heart: All that my heart sees faith and value in
like a sickness: as though I were ill
discourse: talk
anon: later
overbear your will: overrule your wishes
eternally be knit: married
for the ... worn: as it is now quite late
Our purposed hunting ... set aside: The hunting we proposed to do shall be abandoned
Three and three: three men, three women
solemnity: celebrations

	Without the peril of the Athenian law–	
EGEUS	Enough, enough, my lord, you have enough:	
	I beg the law, the law, upon his head.	

Without the peril of the Athenian law–

EGEUS   Enough, enough, my lord, you have enough:
I beg the law, the law, upon his head.
They would have stolen away, they would,
        Demetrius,
Thereby to have defeated you and me,
You of your wife, and me of my consent,
Of my consent that she should be your wife.

DEMETRIUS   My lord, fair Helen told me of their stealth,   160
Of this their purpose hither to this wood;
And I in fury hither followed them,
Fair Helena in fancy following me.
But, my good lord, I wot not by what power–
But by some power it is–my love to Hermia,
Melted as the snow, seems to me now
As the remembrance of an idle gaud,
Which in my childhood I did dote upon.
And all the faith, the virtue of my heart,
The object and the pleasure of mine eye,   170
Is only Helena. To her, my lord,
Was I betrothed ere I saw Hermia;
But, like a sickness, did I loathe this food;
But, as in health, come to my natural taste,
Now I do wish it, love it, long for it,
And will for evermore be true to it.

THESEUS   Fair lovers, you are fortunately met.
Of this discourse we more will hear anon.
Egeus, I will overbear your will;
For in the temple, by and by, with us   180
These couples shall eternally be knit.
And, for the morning now is something worn,
Our purposed hunting shall be set aside.
Away with us to Athens, three and three,
We'll hold a feast in great solemnity.
Come Hippolyta.   [*Exeunt Theseus, Hippolyta,*
                                    Egeus, and train

The court and courtiers leave and the four lovers, still in a dream, start to try and work out what has happened. They follow the duke's party. Bottom, in his turn wakes up, still half-remembering the marvels he has experienced. He feels it should be written down as it is both unique and deep. He would like to call it 'Bottom's Dream' and perform it at the end of their play.

parted eye: double vision, unfocused eyes

Mine own and not mine own: The idea is, if you find something it feels as though it is yours, but it doesn't necessarily belong to you.

yet: still

cue: Bottom wakes up thinking he's still at the rehearsal

expound: explain

patched fool: a jester or court fool in patchwork clothes

The eye of man ...: Bottom is left in a very confused state, as the language suggests.

it hath no bottom: it is unfathomable; there is no rational explanation

Peradventure: perhaps

her death: that is, Thisby's death

DEMETRIUS   These things seem small and undistinguishable,
             Like far-off mountains turned into clouds.

HERMIA   Methinks I see these things with parted eye,
             When every thing seem double.

HELENA   So methinks.   190
             And I have found Demetrius like a jewel,
             Mine own, and not mine own.

DEMETRIUS   Are you sure
             That we are awake? It seems to me
             That yet we sleep, we dream. Do not you think
             The duke was here, and bid us follow him?

HERMIA   Yea, and my father.

HELENA   And Hippolyta.

LYSANDER   And he did bid us follow to the temple.

DEMETRIUS   Why then we are awake, let's follow him.
             And by the way let us recount our dreams.   [*Exeunt*

BOTTOM   [*Awaking*] When my cue comes, call me, and I   200
             will answer. My next is, 'Most fair Pyramus'. Heigh-
             ho. Peter Quince! Flute the bellows-mender!
             Snout the tinker! Starveling! God's my life, stolen
             hence, and left me asleep. I have had a most rare
             vision. I have had a dream, past the wit of man to
             say what dream it was. Man is but an ass, if he go
             about to expound this dream. Methought I was—
             there is no man can tell what. Methought I was, and
             methought I had—but man is but a patched fool, if
             he will offer to say what methought I had. The eye
             of man hath not heard, the ear of man hath not   211
             seen, man's hand is not about to taste, his tongue to
             conceive, nor his heart to report, what my dream
             was. I will get Peter Quince to write a ballad of this
             dream; it shall be called Bottom's Dream, because it
             hath no bottom; and I will sing it in the latter end of
             our play, before the duke. Peradventure, to make it
             the more gracious, I shall sing it at her death.   218
                                                          [*Exit*

Bottom's four friends have been looking for him
without success. They are very despondent because
without him there will not be a play. They are also
regretting the loss of the money the duke might have
given them. Suddenly Bottom arrives.

transported: carried away, kidnapped
marred: spoiled
It goes not forward: It can't be put on
discharge: play the part of
wit: brain
the best person: most suitable figure
paramour: lover
paragon: pattern of excellence
thing of naught: a shameful thing
If our sport had gone forward: If our play had gone
    ahead
we had ... made men: our fortunes would have been
    made.
Thus hath ... life: Snug is suggesting that the Duke would
    have been so taken with Bottom's performance that he
    would have granted him a life-pension of sixpence a day.
    This would have been more than he could have earned at
    his trade.
scaped: failed to receive
courageous: splendid

SCENE **2**

Quince's house

Enter QUINCE, FLUTE, SNOUT, *and* STARVELING

QUINCE   Have you sent to Bottom's house? Is he come
            home yet?

STARVELING He cannot be heard of. Out of doubt he is
            transported.

FLUTE   If he come not, then the play is marred. It goes
            not forward, doth it?

QUINCE   It is not possible. You have not a man in all
            Athens able to discharge Pyramus but he.

FLUTE   No, he hath simply the best wit of any handicraft
            man in Athens.   10

QUINCE   Yea, and the best person too; and he is a very
            paramour for a sweet voice.

FLUTE   You must say 'paragon'. A paramour is, God
            bless us, a thing of naught.

            Enter SNUG

SNUG   Masters, the duke is coming from the temple,
            and there is two or three lords and ladies more
            married. If our sport had gone forward, we had
            all been made men.

FLUTE   O sweet bully Bottom. Thus hath he lost
            sixpence a day during his life; he could not have
            'scaped sixpence a day. An the duke had not
            given him sixpence a day for playing Pyramus,
            I'll be hanged. He would have deserved it.
            Sixpence a day in Pyramus, or nothing.   24

            Enter BOTTOM

BOTTOM   Where are these lads? Where are these hearts?

QUINCE   Bottom! O most courageous day! O most happy
            hour!

Bottom promises to tell them what happened, but for the moment the play is the important thing. They must hurry and get ready.

discourse: tell, speak of
right as it fell out: exactly as it happened
apparel: costumes
strings: strings to tie false beards on with
pumps: dancing shoes
presently: straight away
preferred: short-listed

ACTIVITIES

Keeping track

1 While Titania is under the influence of the drug, what does she give up easily to Oberon?
2 In line 136 what 'choice' does Theseus mean?
3 Who goes hunting in the wood at dawn, and whom do they discover? (lines 103-131).
4 When the lovers wake up, who is in love with whom?
5 What does Theseus announce shall happen when he marries Hippolyta? (lines 179-185)
6 Apart from the ass's head, what other piece of

BOTTOM   Masters, I am to discourse wonders, but ask me
           not what; for if I tell you, I am not true   29
           Athenian. I will tell you every thing, right as it
           fell out.

QUINCE   Let us hear, sweet Bottom.

BOTTOM   Not a word of me. All that I will tell you is, that
           the duke hath dined. Get your apparel together,
           good strings to your beards, new ribbons to your
           pumps, meet presently at the palace, every man
           look o'er his part. For the short and the long is,
           our play is preferred. In any case let Thisby have
           clean linen; and let not him that plays the lion
           pare his nails, for they shall hang out for the   40
           lion's claws. And most dear actors, eat no onions
           nor garlic, for we are to utter sweet breath; and I
           do not doubt but to hear them say, it is a sweet
           comedy. No more words. Away, go away!
           [*Exeunt*

headwear had Oberon seen Bottom wearing? (lines 51-52).
7 What is the good news that Bottom gives his friends when
   he is reunited with them?

Drama

Group work
1 In a performance actors would have to convey the
   workers' worries about Bottom's absence and then, joy at
   his appearance.
   ● Read to yourself the section of Act 4 scene 2 from lines
     1 to 32.

- Cast the parts.
- Read the extract aloud.
- Discuss how to say the lines to convey what the characters are feeling.
- Practise the reading .
- Read it aloud to the rest of the class.

2 Bottom returns to Athens and to his friends.
  - Decide which part you will each play.
  - Improvise Bottom's breathless entry into a second rehearsal under Quince's direction
  - What story does he tell – how do the others react?
  - When you have roughed it out, discuss what is working and what improvements you can make.
  - Rehearse until you each know exactly what to do.
  - Show it to other groups.

3 Without having horses or hounds, how can you create a royal hunt scene? You may wish to make it a modern version.
  - Discuss it in your group.
  - Decide which part you will each play.
  - Form yourselves into a still image showing the hunt.
  - Try 'unfreezing' it for ten seconds with sounds.
  - Elect one person to stand outside and watch it, then make comments on what is effective.
  - Modify your version and practise it.
  - Show it to another group.

4 Take the sequence of events from Egeus finding the lovers (line 128), to the departure of Theseus and Hippolyta (line 186).
  - Following the instructions of the previous exercise, act out the events in the style of a silent movie.
  - Pay great attention to what everyone does at each moment.

Discussion

Scene 1

1 At the beginning of the scene, Bottom is offered all sorts of 'treats' he does not really want. On the other hand there are things that he would like instead. If you were transported into the world of Titania and Oberon, which things would you miss particularly?

2 Look carefully at Oberon's speech beginning, 'Welcome, good Robin …' What do you think his real feelings are about:
   ● Bottom
   ● Titania
   ● gaining the child he wants as his attendant?

3 Theseus and Hippolyta arrive in the forest during the scene. We haven't seen them since Act 1. Do you notice any change in their relationship?

4 When Helena and Demetrius awake, they are still under the influence of magic. Do you think that they would be able to live 'happily ever after' without its influence? What are your reasons for thinking this?

Scene 2

5 Quince, Flute, Snout, and Starveling are at last reunited with Bottom in this scene. What do you think their true feelings are about:
   ● Bottom
   ● the play
   ● the Athenian Court?

Character

Bottom

Scene 1 lines 1-39
Even though transformed into an ass, Bottom is still Bottom in every way. In which ways do his character traits show through in this short scene?

Scene 2 lines 1-24
Here Quince and the other workmen discuss Bottom.
What do they say about him? From this what do you find
out about their feelings towards him?

Oberon

Lines 46-70
From these lines, which of Oberon's characteristics do
you find:
- unlikeable
- likeable

Titania

Lines 75- 102
How does Titania react to the revelation that she had
been in love with an ass? What does this suggest about
her character?

Theseus

Lines 137-140
What aspects of Theseus' character are revealed in these
few lines?

Writing

1 Bottom promises to tell 'everything right as it fell out'.
   What do you think he remembers? Write his version of
   the night from his point of view. Use the sort of
   language you think Bottom might use.
2 At the end of the scene the mechanicals set off to
   perform their play. What do you think goes through
   their minds? Write their thoughts from the point of
   view of one of them as they set off for the Duke's
   celebrations.
3 Theseus overrules Hermia's father, Egeus, and says

she can marry Lysander. As Egeus, write a letter to a close family friend, telling your thoughts and feelings about what has happened from the time you took Hermia to the court of Theseus.

4 As a reporter out to make a name for yourself, write the gossip column of the *Athenian Tribune* reporting the discovery of the lovers in the wood and their forthcoming marriage.

Quiz

Who says:
1 'I am to discourse wonders'
2 'If he come not then the play is marred'
3 'O sweet bully Bottom'
4 Who says and to whom 'I know you two are rival enemies'?
5 Who repeats himself six times in as many lines?

Hippolyta and Theseus talk over what they have learnt of the lovers' experiences in the wood. Theseus is inclined to put it all down to imagination. This affects madmen, lovers and poets, all in different ways. But Hippolyta believes there is truth in what they say, as they all tell much the same story.

antique fables: old tales

fairy toys: foolish stories about fairies

shaping fantasies: creative imaginations

apprehend: dream up

Are ... all compact: completely made up of imagination

Helen: famous for her beauty. When she was carried off to Troy by Paris, Priam's son, her husband Menelaus and his allies laid siege to the city for 10 years.

a brow of Egypt: a gypsy's face

bodies forth: gives mental shape to

a local habitation: a real place to live

apprehend: conjure up

It comprehends ... that joy: It must include an imagined bringer of that joy.

But ... admirable: When we look at the whole story of the night's events and the fact that all their minds were affected in an identical way, it points to more than mere imagination and becomes a certainty; but still strange and something to be wondered at.

Act five

Theseus' court

Enter THESEUS, HIPPOLYTA, PHILOSTRATE, LORDS, *and* ATTENDANTS

HIPPOLYTA   'T is strange, my Theseus, that these lovers
             speak of.

THESEUS   More strange than true. I never may believe
             These antique fables, nor these fairy toys.
             Lovers and madmen have such seething brains,
             Such shaping fantasies, that apprehend
             More than cool reason ever comprehends.
             The lunatic, the lover, and the poet
             Are of imagination all compact.
             One see more devils than vast hell can hold,
             That is the madman. The lover, all as frantic,   10
             Sees Helen's beauty in a brow of Egypt.
             The poet's eye, in a fine frenzy rolling,
             Doth glance from heaven to earth, from earth to
                heaven;
             And as imagination bodies forth
             The forms of things unknown, the poet's pen
             Turns them to shapes, and gives to airy nothing
             A local habitation and a name.
             Such tricks hath strong imagination,
             That if it would but apprehend some joy,
             It comprehends some bringer of that joy;   20
             Or in the night, imagining some fear,
             How easy is a bush supposed a bear!

HIPPOLYTA   But all the story of the night told over,
             And all their minds transfigured so together,
             More witnesseth than fancy's images,
             And grows to something of great constancy;

The happy lovers come in. The weddings have taken place and the duke now wants to choose a suitable entertainment for the evening. Philostrate, who has organised a list of possible performances, hands it to Theseus. He has some reason for rejecting everything on the list until he comes to the title of the workmen's play.

1 Lysander, speaking for the lovers, returns Theseus' greeting.

2 Theseus asks what entertainment to order for the evening. He would like a play and calls Philostrate, who is in charge, to tell him what the choice is.

3 Theseus considers the list offered to him and rejects several items, either because he has seen them before or because they do not suit the mood after a wedding. He is then attracted by the contradictions in the description of the workmen's play.

But howsoever, strange and admirable.

THESEUS   Here come the lovers, full of joy and mirth.

Enter LYSANDER, DEMETRIUS, HERMIA, *and* HELENA

Joy, gentle friends, joy and fresh days of love
Accompany your hearts!

LYSANDER   More than to us   30
Wait in your royal walks, your board, your bed.

THESEUS   Come now; what masques, what dances shall we
      have,
To wear away this long age of three hours
Between our after-supper and bed-time?
Where is our usual manager of mirth?
What revels are in hand? Is there no play,
To ease the anguish of a torturing hour?
Call Philostrate.

PHILOSTRATE   Here mighty Theseus.

THESEUS   Say, what abridgement have you for this evening?
What masque, what music? How shall we beguile   40
The lazy time, if not with some delight?

PHILOSTRATE There is a brief how many sports are ripe.
Make choice of which your highness will see first.
                                [Gives a paper

THESEUS   ' The battle with the Centaurs, to be sung
By an Athenian eunuch to the harp.'
We'll none of that. That have I told my love,
In glory of my kinsman Hercules.
' The riot of the tipsy Bacchanals,
Tearing the Thracian singer in their rage.'
That is an old device, and it was played   50
When I from Thebes came last a conqueror.
' The thrice three Muses mourning for the death
Of learning, late deceased in beggary.'
That is some satire, keen and critical,
Not sorting with a nuptial ceremony.
'A tedious brief scene of young Pyramus

Philostrate agrees with the description 'tedious and brief' and explains that the play is being put on by men who have never put on a performance before. He is concerned that they will find it comic instead of tragic. However, this is the play Theseus wants to see, and even Hippolyta's fears cannot put him off.

4

4　Philostrate, who says he has seen a rehearsal, tries to put them off. There were tears of laughter in his eyes when he watched it and he is afraid that they will make fun of the men who have worked so hard to entertain them.

amiss: wrong
simpleness: innocence
wretchedness: lack of ability
o'ercharged: overburdened. Hippolyta is afraid she will see these men who are below her socially and intellectually doing something far too ambitious which will mean that they will fail in their attempt to please the duke.

And his love Thisby; very tragical mirth.'
Merry and tragical? Tedious and brief?
That is, hot ice and wondrous strange snow.
How shall we find the concord of this discord? 60

PHILOSTRATE A play there is, my lord, some ten words long,
Which is as brief as I have known a play;
But by ten words, my lord, it is too long,
Which makes it tedious. For in all the play
There is not one word apt, one player fitted.
And tragical, my noble lord, it is;
For Pyramus therein doth kill himself.
Which when I saw rehearsed, I must confess,
Made mine eyes water. But more merry tears
The passion of loud laughter never shed. 70

THESEUS What are they that do play it?

PHILOSTRATE Hard-handed men, that work in Athens here,
Which never laboured in their minds till now;
And now have toiled their unbreathed memories
With this same play, against your nuptial.

THESEUS And we will hear it.

PHILOSTRATE   No my noble lord,
It is not for you. I have heard it over,
And it is nothing, nothing in the world;
Unless you can find sport in their intents,
Extremely stretched and conned with cruel pain, 80
To do you service.

THESEUS   I will hear that play.
For never anything can be amiss,
When simpleness and duty tender it.
Go, bring them in, and take your places, ladies.
                           [*Exit Philostrate*

HIPPOLYTA I love not to see wretchedness o'ercharged,
And duty in his service perishing.

THESEUS Why gentle sweet, you shall see no such thing.

HIPPOLYTA He says they can do nothing in this kind.

Theseus has often had to listen to speeches of
welcome from people who have rehearsed them
thoroughly and then suffer so much from stage fright
that they cannot deliver them properly. He still saw
their efforts as a welcome, and will do so again.
The play begins with a prologue spoken by Quince. It
is wrongly punctuated, and so often says the opposite
of what it means.

The kinder we: then we shall be all the more generous
sport: entertainment
take what they mistake: understand what they
    misunderstand
Takes ... not merit: their intentions rather than their
    achievement
clerks: scholars
purposed: planned
premeditated welcomes: well-prepared speeches of
    welcome
Make periods ... sentences: put full-stops in the middle
    of sentences (exactly as in the Prologue to come, lines
    108-117 where this creates nonsense and comedy)
rattling: chattering
saucy: impertinent
audacious: bold
to my capacity: as far as I am concerned
addressed: ready to begin
in despite: against your wishes
minding: meaning
stand upon points: bother about punctuation
rid: a pun as it means both 'got rid of' and 'ridden'
stop: means both 'the horse coming to a halt' and 'full-
    stop'
true: properly

THESEUS   The kinder we, to give them thanks for nothing.
          Our sport shall be to take what they mistake;   90
          And what poor duty cannot do, noble respect
          Takes it in might, not merit.
          Where I have come, great clerks have purposed
          To greet me with premeditated welcomes;
          Where I have seen them shiver and look pale,
          Make periods in the midst of sentences,
          Throttle their practised accent in their fears,
          And in conclusion dumbly have broke off,
          Not paying me a welcome. Trust me sweet,
          Out of this silence yet I picked a welcome;   100
          And in the modesty of fearful duty
          I read as much as from the rattling tongue
          Of saucy and audacious eloquence.
          Love, therefore, and tongue-tied simplicity
          In least speak most, to my capacity.

          Enter PHILOSTRATE

PHILOSTRATE So please your grace, the prologue is addressed.
THESEUS   Let him approach.   [*Flourish of trumpets*

          Enter QUINCE *as* PROLOGUE

PROLOGUE If we offend, it is with our good will.
          That you should think, we come not to offend,
          But with good will. To show our simple skill,   110
          That is the true beginning of our end.
          Consider then, we come but in despite.
          We do not come, as minding to content you,
          Our true intent is. All for your delight
          We are not here. That you should here repent you,
          The actors are at hand; and by their show,
          You shall know all, that you are like to know.
THESEUS   This fellow doth not stand upon points.
LYSANDER He hath rid his prologue like a rough colt; he
          knows not the stop. A good moral, my lord: it is

The duke and duchess comment on the prologue which continues by telling the story of the whole play, indicating who is to play each character.

in government: under control
impaired: damaged
Gentles: Ladies and Gentlemen
sunder: separate, keep apart
hight: is called
mantle: cloak
fall: let fall, drop
tall: handsome
broached: pierced
tarrying: waiting
At large discourse: speak at length

| | not enough to speak, but to speak true. | 121 |

HIPPOLYTA Indeed he hath played on his prologue like a child
on a recorder, a sound, but not in government.

THESEUS His speech was like a tangled chain; nothing
impaired, but all disordered. Who is next?

Enter PYRAMUS *and* THISBY, WALL, MOONSHINE, *and*
LION

PROLOGUE Gentles, perchance you wonder at this show,
     But wonder on, till truth make all things plain.
This man is Pyramus, if you would know;
     This beauteous lady Thisby is certain.
This man, with lime and rough-cast, doth
     present   130
     Wall, that vile Wall which did these lovers sunder;
And through Wall's chink, poor souls, they are
     content
     To whisper. At the which let no man wonder.
This man, with lanthorn, dog, and bush of thorn,
     Presenteth Moonshine. For if you will know,
By moonshine did these lovers think no scorn
     To meet at Ninus' tomb, there, there to woo.
This grisly beast, which Lion hight by name,
The trusty Thisby, coming first by night,
Did scare away, or rather did affright.   140
And as she fled, her mantle she did fall,
     Which Lion vile with bloody mouth did stain.
Anon comes Pyramus, sweet youth, and tall,
     And finds his trusty Thisby's mantle slain.
Whereat, with blade, with bloody blameful blade,
     He bravely broached his boiling bloody breast.
And Thisby, tarrying in mulberry shade,
     His dagger drew, and died. For all the rest,
Let Lion, Moonshine, Wall, and lovers twain
At large discourse, while here they do remain. 150
          [*Exeunt Prologue, Pyramus, Thisby, Lion, and
                                             Moonshine*

**Snout, playing the wall, explains his part. Bottom, as
Pyramus, speaks first to the night, and then to the
wall.**

interlude: play
befall: happen
sinister: left
wittiest partition: most intelligent wall
Jove shield you: may God protect you

THESEUS	I wonder if the lion be to speak.
DEMETRIUS	No wonder, my lord. One lion may, when many asses do.
WALL	In this same interlude it doth befall
	That I, one Snout by name, present a wall;
	And such a wall, as I would have you think,
	That had in it a crannied hole or chink,
	Through which the lovers, Pyramus and Thisby,
	Did whisper often very secretly.
	This loam, this rough-cast, and this stone doth show 160
	That I am that same wall; the truth is so.
	And this the cranny is, right and sinister,
	Through which the fearful lovers are to whisper.
THESEUS	Would you desire lime and hair to speak better?
DEMETRIUS	It is the wittiest partition, that ever I heard discourse, my lord.

Enter PYRAMUS

THESEUS	Pyramus draws near the wall: silence!
PYRAMUS	O grim-looked night! O night with hue so black!
	O night, which ever art when day is not!
	O night, O night, alack, alack, alack, 170
	I fear my Thisby's promise is forgot!
	And thou, O wall, O sweet, O lovely wall,
	That stand'st between her father's ground and mine!
	Thou wall, O wall, O sweet and lovely wall,
	Show me thy chink, to blink through with mine eyne!
	[*Wall holds up his fingers*
	Thanks, courteous wall. Jove shield thee well for this.
	But what see I? No Thisby do I see.
	O wicked wall, through whom I see no bliss,
	Cursed be thy stones for thus deceiving me!

Bottom corrects the duke when he jokingly makes a comment on the play. Thisby and Pyramus declare their love through the chink in the wall. The lovers and the duke and duchess continue to comment.

sensible: able to have feelings

No ... wall: Bottom comes out of character and speaks to his audience.

fall pat: turn out exactly

Limander: Bottom means Leander, who in the Greek myth was drowned trying to swim the Hellespont to reach his love, Hero.

Helen: used mistakenly for Hero

Fates: the three sisters who in Greek mythology control our birth, life and death.

as Shafalus to Procrus: mistakes for another pair of tragic lovers, Cephalus and Procris.

Ninny's tomb: see note on Act 3 scene 1 line 90. Bottom is still saying Ninny for Ninus.

Tide life, tide death: come life, come death

discharged: carried out, performed

mural: wall

No remedy: There is nothing to be done

in this kind: actors

amend them: improve on them

THESEUS	The wall methinks, being sensible, should curse again. 181
PYRAMUS	No in truth, sir, he should not. 'Deceiving me' is Thisby's cue. She is to enter now, and I am to spy her through the wall. You shall see, it will fall pat as I told you. Yonder she comes.

Enter THISBY

THISBY	O wall, full often hast thou heard my moans,
	    For parting my fair Pyramus and me!
	My cherry lips have often kissed thy stones,
	    Thy stones with lime and hair knit up in thee.

PYRAMUS	I see a voice; now will I to the chink, 190 To spy an I can hear my Thisby's face. Thisby!
THISBY	My love thou art my love, I think.
PYRAMUS	Think what thou wilt, I am thy lover's grace, And, like Limander, am I trusty still.
THISBY	And I like Helen, till the Fates me kill.
PYRAMUS	Not Shafalus to Procrus was so true.
THISBY	As Shafalus to Procrus, I to you.
PYRAMUS	O kiss me through the hole of this vile wall.
THISBY	I kiss the wall's hole, not your lips at all. 199
PYRAMUS	Wilt thou at Ninny's tomb meet me straightway?
THISBY	'Tide life, 'tide death, I come without delay. [*Exeunt Pyramus and Thisby*
WALL	Thus have I, Wall, my part discharged so; And, being done, thus Wall away doth go. [*Exit*
THESEUS	Now is the mural down between the two neighbours.
DEMETRIUS	No remedy my lord, when walls are so wilful to hear without warning.
HIPPOLYTA	This is the silliest stuff that ever I heard.
THESEUS	The best in this kind are but shadows; and the worst are no worse, if imagination amend them. 210

The lion and the moon enter and explain themselves
to the audience as planned, while the members of the
audience make witty comments to one another.

---

perchance: perhaps
fell: fierce and also (lion)skin
dam: mother Snug must be a male, not a female lion!
in strife: aggressively
'twere pity on my life: my life would be at risk
good conscience: sound judgement
valour: bravery. Foxes are known for their slyness or
  cunning rather than bravery.
discretion: sound judgement. Geese are known for their
  silliness not for good judgement.
lanthorn: lantern
horned: crescent or new moon, which looks like two horns
He ... head: the mark of a man with an unfaithful wife
He ... circumference: Because he is representing a full
  moon, there are no horns to be seen.
man i' th' moon: it is supposed to be possible to make out
  a face in the marks you can see on the moon's surface.
in snuff: about to go out.

HIPPOLYTA	It must be your imagination then, and not theirs.
THESEUS	If we imagine no worse of them than they of themselves, they may pass for excellent men. Here come two noble beasts in, a moon and a lion.

Enter LION *and* MOONSHINE

LION	You ladies, you, whose gentle hearts do fear

    The smallest monstrous mouse that creeps on floor,
May now perchance both quake and tremble here.
    When lion rough in wildest rage doth roar.
Then know that I, as Snug the joiner am
A lion fell, nor else no lion's dam;   220
For if I should as lion come in strife
Into this place, 't were pity on my life.

THESEUS	A very gentle beast, and of a good conscience.
DEMETRIUS	The very best at a beast, my lord, that e'er I saw.
LYSANDER	This lion is a very fox for his valour.
THESEUS	True; and a goose for his discretion.
DEMETRIUS	Not so my lord, for his valour cannot carry his discretion, and the fox carries the goose.
THESEUS	His discretion, I am sure, cannot carry his valour; for the goose carries not the fox. It is well. Leave it to his discretion, and let us listen to the moon. 232
MOONSHINE	This lanthorn doth the horned moon present–
DEMETRIUS	He should have worn the horns on his head.
THESEUS	He is no crescent, and his horns are invisible within the circumference.
MOONSHINE	This lanthorn doth the horned moon present, Myself the man i' th' moon do seem to be.
THESEUS	This is the greatest error of all the rest; the man should be put into the lanthorn. How is it else the man i' th' moon? 241
DEMETRIUS	He dares not come there for the candle. For you see, it is already in snuff.

The story of the play proceeds, still with comments from the audience. Thisby goes to Ninus' tomb to meet Pyramus, but before he arrives a lion frightens her away, but savages her cloak, which Pyramus finds.

---

must stay the time: see the whole play through
Well moused: the lion shakes Thisby's cloak in his jaws as a cat shakes a mouse.
mark: pay attention

HIPPOLYTA	I am aweary of this moon. Would he would change.
THESEUS	It appears by his small light of discretion, that he is in the wane. But yet, in courtesy, in all reason, we must stay the time.
LYSANDER	Proceed Moon.
MOONSHINE	All that I have to say, is to tell you that the lanthorn is the moon, I the man in the moon, this thorn-bush, my thorn-bush, and this dog my dog. 251
DEMETRIUS	Why all these should be in the lanthorn; for all these are in the moon. But silence, here comes Thisby.

Enter THISBY

THISBY	This is old Ninny's tomb. Where is my love?
LION	[*Roars*] Oh– [*Thisby runs off*
DEMETRIUS	Well roared, Lion.
THESEUS	Well run, Thisby.
HIPPOLYTA	Well shone, Moon. Truly the moon shines with a good grace. [*The Lion shakes Thisby's mantle, and exit*
THESEUS	Well moused, Lion. 261
DEMETRIUS	And then came Pyramus.
LYSANDER	And so the lion vanished.

Enter PYRAMUS

PYRAMUS	Sweet moon, I thank thee for thy sunny beams.
	I thank thee, moon, for shining now so bright.
	For by thy gracious, golden, glittering gleams,
	I trust to take of truest Thisby sight.
	But stay, O spite!
	But mark, poor knight,
	What dreadful dole is here! 270
	Eyes do you see?
	How can it be?
	O dainty duck! O dear!

Pyramus finds blood on the cloak and assumes that something dreadful has happened to Thisby. Overcome with grief, he stabs himself.

Furies: In Greek mythology they were three fierce goddesses who carried out the curses made on murderers and other criminals

thrum: each length of the warp thread on a weaving-loom. It is used here for alliteration.

Quail: overcome

quell: put to death. The alliteration is more important for the comic effect than the sense.

passion: grief, outburst

Beshrew: curse

frame: create

deflowered: violated

dame: lady

cheer: cheerfulness

pap: breast

hop: beat

die: a die is the singular form of dice i.e. one die, two dice. It is used here as a pun to comment on Pyramus' long-drawn-out death.

ace: one spot on a die. Ace too becomes a pun, with reference to 'ass', which is also dramatic irony, since only we know that Bottom was given an ass's head in the wood.

passion: passionate speech

	Thy mantle good,
	What, stained with blood!
	Approach ye Furies fell.
	O Fates, come, come,
	Cut thread and thrum,
	Quail, crush, conclude, and quell.
THESEUS	This passion, and the death of a dear friend, 280
	would go near to make a man look sad.
HIPPOLYTA	Beshrew my heart, but I pity the man.
PYRAMUS	O wherefore Nature, didst thou lions frame?
	Since lion vile hath here deflowered my dear.
	Which is–no, no–which was the fairest dame
	That lived, that loved, that liked, that looked
	with cheer.
	Come tears, confound.
	Out sword, and wound
	The pap of Pyramus;
	Ay, that left pap, 290
	Where heart doth hop. *[Stabs himself*
	Thus die I, thus, thus, thus
	Now am I dead,
	Now am I fled,
	My soul is in the sky.
	Tongue lose thy light,
	Moon take thy flight, *[Exit Moonshine*
	Now die, die, die, die, die. *[Dies*
DEMETRIUS	No die, but an ace for him; for he is but one.
LYSANDER	Less than an ace, man; for he is dead, he is nothing. 300
THESEUS	With the help of a surgeon he might yet recover,
	and prove an ass.
HIPPOLYTA	How chance Moonshine is gone before Thisby
	comes back and finds her lover?
THESEUS	She will find him by starlight. Here she comes,
	and her passion ends the play.

Enter THISBY

Thisby at first assumes her lover is asleep, but finding he is dead, mourns him in a long speech and then stabs herself to death. Bottom explains the end of the play and then offers an epilogue or a dance.

mote: the least little thing (mote means speck of dust)
warrant: keep, protect
means: laments, mourns
videlicet: a Latin legal term – namely
Sisters Three: the Fates.
shore: shorn, cut
gore: blood
imbrue: stain with blood
epilogue: a speech to the audience at the end of the play
Bergamask: a country dance from Bergamo in Italy

HIPPOLYTA   Methinks she should not use a long one for such
             a Pyramus. I hope she will be brief.

DEMETRIUS   A mote will turn the balance, which Pyramus,
             which Thisby, is the better; he for a man, God
             warrant us; she for a woman, God bless us.   311

LYSANDER   She hath spied him already with those sweet eyes.

DEMETRIUS   And thus she means, videlicet–

THISBY   Asleep my love?
                 What, dead, my dove?
             O Pyramus, arise.
                 Speak, speak. Quite dumb?
                 Dead, dead? A tomb
             Must cover thy sweet eyes.
                 These lily lips,   320
                 This cherry nose,
             These yellow cowslip cheeks,
                 Are gone, are gone.
                 Lovers, make moan.
             His eyes were green as leeks.
                 O Sisters Three,
                 Come, come to me,
             With hands as pale as milk;
                 Lay them in gore,
                 Since you have shore   330
             With shears his thread of silk.
                 Tongue, not a word.
                 Come, trusty sword;
             Come blade, my breast imbrue.   [*Stabs herself*
                 And farewell, friends,
                 Thus Thisby ends
             Adieu, adieu, adieu.   [*Dies*

THESEUS   Moonshine and Lion are left to bury the dead.

DEMETRIUS   Ay, and Wall too.   339

BOTTOM   [*Starting up*] No, I assure you, the wall is down
             that parted their fathers. Will it please you to see
             the epilogue, or to hear a Bergamask dance

Theseus asks for the dance and praises their play. The workmen dance (and presumably leave). Theseus says it is past midnight and time for bed. They can look forward to a fortnight of celebrations.

When the humans have gone Puck comes in. Night is the time for spirits and he has been sent, with broom in hand, to get things ready.

---

writ: wrote

discharged: performed

tongue: the clapper of the bell striking midnight

out-sleep: oversleep

overwatched: stayed up too late

palpable-gross: plainly stupid

beguiled: charmed away

gait: pace

solemnity: celebration of our wedding

revels: entertainments

behowls: howls at

heavy: tired

foredone: exhausted

wasted brands: burnt-out wood (on the fire)

Puts ... shroud: Makes someone lying tossing and turning in bed think of death.

Every one ... sprite: Each grave opens up to let its ghost out

Hecate: Greek goddess associated with night and with hell, with ghosts and magic. Often shown as three statues in one.

frolic: playful

hallowed: blessed

between two of our company?

THESEUS No epilogue, I pray you; for your plays needs no
excuse. Never excuse; for when the players are
all dead, there need none be blamed. Marry if he
that writ it had played Pyramus, and hanged
himself in Thisby's garter, it would have been a
fine tragedy. And so it is, truly, and very notably
discharged. But come, your Bergamask. Let your
epilogue alone.   [*A dance*   351
The iron tongue of midnight hath told twelve.
Lovers to bed, 'tis almost fairy time.
I fear we shall out-sleep the coming morn,
As much as we this night have overwatched.
This palpable-gross play hath well beguiled
The heavy gait of night. Sweet friends, to bed.
A fortnight hold we this solemnity,
In nightly revels, and new jollity.   [*Exeunt*

Enter PUCK

PUCK   Now the hungry lion roars,   360
                    And the wolf behowls the moon;
                Whilst the heavy ploughman snores,
                    All with weary task fordone.
                Now the wasted brands do glow,
                    Whilst the screech-owl, screeching loud,
                Puts the wretch that lies in woe
                    In remembrance of a shroud.
                Now it is the time of night,
                    That the graves all gaping wide,
                Every one lets forth his sprite,   370
                    In the church-way paths to glide.
                And we fairies, that do run
                    By the triple Hecate's team,
                From the presence of the sun,
                    Following darkness like a dream,
                Now are frolic: not a mouse
                Shall disturb this hallowed house.

Oberon and Titania enter with all their attendants, ready, as promised, to sing and dance and bless the palace and the newly-weds sleeping in it. They promise true love and happiness, and children born without any disfigurement. They will dance there until daybreak.

glimmering light: faint, wavering light
ditty: song
trippingly: lightly
rehearse: repeat
by rote: from memory
stray: wander
issue: children
blots of Nature's hand: deformities, accidents of birth
mark prodigious: monstrous birthmark
nativity: birth
take his gait: make his way
several: separate
make no stay: don't delay

I am sent with broom before,
To sweep the dust behind the door.   379

Enter OBERON *and* TITANIA *with their train*

OBERON   Through the house give glimmering light,
By the dead and drowsy fire,
Every elf and fairy sprite
Hop as light as bird from briar,
And this ditty after me,
Sing, and dance it trippingly.

TITANIA   First rehearse your song by rote,
To each word a warbling note.
Hand in hand, with fairy grace,
Will we sing, and bless this place.   [*Song and dance*

OBERON   Now, until the break of day,   390
Through this house each fairy stray.
To the best bride-bed will we,
Which by us shall blessed be.
And the issue there create,
Ever shall be fortunate.
So shall all the couples three
Ever true in loving be;
And the blots of Nature's hand
Shall not in their issue stand.
Never mole, hare lip, nor scar,   400
Nor mark prodigious, such as are
Despised in nativity,
Shall upon their children be.
With this field-dew consecrate,
Every fairy take his gait,
And each several chamber bless,
Through this palace, with sweet peace;
And the owner of it blest,
Ever shall in safety rest.
Trip away; make no stay;
Meet me all by break of day.   410
                    [*Exeunt Oberon, Titania, and train*

Puck gives the epilogue. It is an apology for any
offence given, and a suggestion that the audience, too,
has in fact been dreaming. He asks for the audience's
goodwill and wishes them goodnight.

shadows: fairies, spirits
No more yielding but: offering no more than
reprehend: find fault with us
mend: do better
unearned luck: luck we have not deserved
scape: escape
serpent's tongue: hisses from the audience
Give me your hands: clap, applaud us
restore amends: make improvements

ACTIVITIES

Keeping track

1 Where does this scene take place and what is the
  special occasion?
2 Name the official guests.
3 Which part does each 'rude mechanical' play?
4 Who says 'Our sport shall be to take what they
  mistake?' What does it mean?
5 What is the story of 'Pyramus and Thisby'? Does it
  remind you of any other love stories?
6 What does Puck mean, in the play's final lines when
  he says:

EPILOGUE

PUCK   If we shadows have offended,
Think but this, and all is mended,
That you have but slumbered here,
While these visions did appear.
And this weak and idle theme,
No more yielding but a dream,
Gentles, do not reprehend.
If you pardon, we will mend.
And, as I am an honest Puck,   420
If we have unearned luck
Now to 'scape the serpent's tongue,
We will make amends ere long;
Else the Puck a liar call.
So, good night unto you all.
Give me your hands, if we be friends,
And Robin shall restore amends.   [*Exit*

'Give me your hands, if we be friends....'?
Can you think of more than one meaning to this?

Discussion

1 Why do you think that Shakespeare wanted to include a
story with a wall in it? What is it intended to symbolise?
Look for evidence of this symbolism in the scene and in the
play.
2 Imagine that we had not heard the opinions of the invited
guests, at the beginning of the scene. What stage directions

might Shakespeare have given the actors, to ensure that we the audience were able to understand how the guests felt about the play shortly to be performed?

3 Do you think that Shakespeare is being insensitive in Oberon's lines 395-400?

4 Do you think that this play has a good title? Why do you think Shakespeare called it a 'dream'? Support your opinion with evidence from the scene and from the whole play.

5 Some stories can be said to have a 'moral'. What does this mean? Do you think there is a 'moral' to *A Midsummer Night's Dream*? (Or is there more than one?)

Character

1 What do we learn of Theseus and Hippolyta's characters in this scene? (lines 85-105 and 118-125)

2 From the comments that they make during the performance by Quince, Bottom and the others, what extra insights do we get into the character of the lovers?

3 Detail the changes of relationships between Helena, Hermia, Demetrius and Lysander since the beginning of the play. Prepare a grid to indicate in which act and scene the changes occur. Also include the reasons for these changes. Use your Character logs to help you.

4 Earlier in the play, Puck was said to enjoy his mischievousness. Is there evidence of this here? What other aspects of his character can you identify?

5 Use your Character logs to explore how (if at all) the characters of Oberon and Titania have changed since the beginning of the play. How would you describe their present relationship?

6 Why do you think Shakespeare chose Puck to close the play? Write an alternative to Puck's last speech – the Epilogue. Should he be the one to say it? Give your reasons.

7 Close your Character logs for each character.

Drama

In groups.

1 We hear very little about what the audience other than Theseus and Hippolyta says during the play's performance. Script the conversation between Helena, Hermia, Demetrius and Lysander.

2 Through improvisation, develop a five minute play which is to be presented to a royal gathering by either: a Sunday school group or a modern group of workmen.

 ● Decide on the story (you may find it best to choose a well-known one with which you are all familiar).
 ● Choose who will take each part.
 ● Decide the important moments that must be included.
 ● Walk these through.
 ● Discuss what is successful.
 ● Go over the scene until everyone is confident about what they do at each moment.
 ● Present it to other groups.

3 Select five key moments from this act and make a still image of each one in sequence.

 Select a member of the group to invent a caption for each still image after you have made it.

In pairs.

4 Play out Hermia and Helena's possible conversation, as they meet before the evening's celebration.

5 Now do the same thing, but with Lysander and Demetrius.

Close study

1 In previous scenes you have been asked to look carefully at rhythm and rhyming patterns used by characters, at certain times in the play. Who speaks in verse in this scene? Make a note of the lines and who says them.

2 Look at the words Theseus says to Hippolyta (lines 89-105). With a partner, work out what he is saying. Does this tell you anything new about his character?

3 Quince is so nervous that he says the opposite of what he means to say in his first speech to the court. (lines 108-117) Read it through and then note down what he was trying to say.

4 Choose several lines from this scene which (in your opinion) are typical examples of 'Shakespearean English'. Translate them into everyday English.

5 If you were given an opportunity to direct the play within the play for television, what instructions would you give the actors and camera crew, at the following points in the scene?

- Theseus, Hippolyta, Philostrate, lords and attendants, at the beginning of the scene.
- As Helena, Hermia, Demetrius and Lysander enter.
- When all of the actors are first on the stage, together.
- The royal couple and guests and the actors, at the end of the scene.

For each of the four points.

- draw a diagram to show where the actors will be
- use arrows to mark their movements, if any
- use a cross to mark the positions of the cameras (keep it simple and use two cameras)
- show their movements, if any, by dotted lines and arrows
- write notes explaining the instructions you would give the actors and the camera crew.

6 Look at Puck's speech lines (361-80).
Make a list, in your own words of the different things he mentions that happen at night.
What impression of the human world and the fairy world does this speech give?

Writing

1 One of the new, young, servants has obtained the services of a scribe to write a letter home to his family describing the experience of the wedding feast, his first banquet. What does he dictate?

2 Your film *A Midsummer Night's Dream* was such a success, that you have been invited to script the sequel *A Midsummer Night's Dream II*. Write a letter to the producer to outline the developments in this sequel.

3 As producer you need to set out your instructions for the costume department. You must include details for all of the characters and your choice of garment should indicate the kind of atmosphere which you would like to create for the audience. Drawings may be included.

4 After the play has been performed, Bottom describes to his family how it was received, particularly describing how he performed. Write what he says.

5 As Hermia or Lysander or Helena or Demetrius, write your secret diary, describing your feelings from the events in the wood to the celebrations at the palace.

6 Write a blessing either for children about to be born or for people about to be married. You may write it either in modern language, or in the style of Shakespeare, with rhyming couplets.

Quiz

1 Are the lovers involved in an 'owl-like' activity?

2 For how long does Theseus expect them to celebrate their marriages?

3 Who says that the play is too long? By how many words is it said to be too long?

4 Which four colours would you need to paint a picture of Pyramus' face as Thisby sees him?

Explorations

Keeping track

When you are studying a play one of the most difficult things to do is to keep track of all the ideas and information you gain as you work on it scene by scene. It is important to keep a note of what you do. Two good ways of organising your work are to keep a Scene log and a Character log.

Scene log

As you work on each scene, make a list of the basic information about it:
● when and where it takes place
● the characters in it
● what happens.
Then add any thoughts and comments you want to remember. You could use the layout illustrated opposite - or you may prefer to make up your own.

Character log

At the same time, you can keep a log for each of the main characters. Use this to record what you find out about the character in every scene he or she appears in:
● key points about the character
● your reasons for choosing these
● the numbers of important lines
● short quotations to back up the key points.
Again there is a layout opposite, but you may prefer your own approach.

Scene Log

Act/ scene	Time/ Place	Characters	Action	Comments
1/1	Athens, the court	Theseus, Hippolyta, Egeus, Hermia, Lysander, Demetrius	Egeus comes to the court to complain about his daughter, Hermia. She wants to marry Lysander. Egeus wants her to marry Demetrius.	Arranged marriages were usual but Egeus does seem very harsh.

Character Log

Character:	*Theseus*			
Act/ scene	**Key points**	**Reasons**	**Key lines**	**Short quotations**
1/1	He is in love. He is sensitive and thoughtful about the celebrations.	He is looking forward, with Hippolyta, to their wedding. He had conquered her in battle and wants to make up for that.	line 3 lines 16–18	O methinks how slow this old moon wanes Hippolyta, I wooed thee with my sword … But I will wed thee in another key.

Drama activities

Most of these activities can be done in small groups or by the class as a whole. They work by slowing down the action of the play and helping you focus on a small section of it - so that you can think more deeply about characters, plot and themes.

Hotseating

Hotseating means putting one of the characters 'under the microscope' at a particular point in the play. This is how it works:

1 Begin by choosing a particular character and a particular moment in the play. For example you might choose Hermia when her father brings her before the duke (Act 1 scene 1).
2 One person (student or teacher) is selected to be the chosen character.
3 That person sits 'in the hotseat', with the rest of the group arranged round in a semi-circle, or a circle.
4 The rest then ask questions about how the character feels, why s/he has acted in that way, and so on. Try to keep the questions going and not to give the person in the hotseat too much time to think.

Variations

1 The questioners themselves take on roles. (In the example above they could be schoolfriends of hers, or her old nurse she has asked for advice).
2 Characters can be hotseated at a series of key moments in a scene to see how their opinions and attitudes change.
3 The questioners can take different attitudes to the character. For example:
   ● aggressive
   ● pleading
   ● disbelieving.

Freeze!

It is very useful to be able to 'stop the action' and concentrate on a single moment in the play. You can do this in a number of ways.

Photographs

Imagine that someone has taken a photograph of a particular moment, or that - as if it were a film or video - the action has been frozen. Once you have chosen the moment, you can work in a number of different ways:

- Act that part of the scene and then 'Freeze!' - you will probably find it easier if you have a 'director' standing outside the scene to shout 'Freeze!'
- Discuss what the photograph should look like and then arrange yourselves into the photograph.
- One at a time place yourself in the photograph; each person 'entering' it must take notice of what is there already.
- Once you have arranged the photograph, take it in turns to come out of it and comment on it, with suggestions for improvements.

There are a number of ways in which you can develop your photograph:

- Each person takes it in turn to speak his/her thoughts at that moment in the scene.
- The photograph is given a caption.
- Some members of the group do not take part in the photograph. Instead they provide a sound track of speech or sound effects, or both.

Statues

Make a statue like this:

1 Select a moment in the play, or a title from the play (for example, 'My mistress with a monster is in love').
2 Choose one member of the group to be the sculptor. That person then arranges the rest of the group, one at a time to make the statue. Statues are different from photographs in

two important ways:
- they are made by a 'sculptor' and tell us about the sculptor's view of the person or event;
- if they talk, they tell us about what they can 'see'. For example if there was a statue of Theseus and Hippolyta as they appeared on their wedding day, it could only 'tell' us about how the citizens of Athens behaved when they saw the statue. If you want Theseus and Hippolyta to speak of their thoughts at that moment, then hotseat them, or make a photograph.

Forum theatre

In Forum theatre, one or two people take on roles and the rest of the group are 'directors'. It works like this:

1 Select a moment in the play. (For example the moment when Demetrius tells Helena he is in love with her.)

2 Select one member of the group to be Demetrius and another Helena.

3 Organise your working area, so that everyone knows where the other characters are, where characters make entrances and exits, and so on.

4 Begin by asking Demetrius and Helena to offer their own first thoughts about position, gesture and movement.

5 The directors then experiment with different ways of presenting that moment. They can:
- ask Demetrius and Helena to take up a particular position, use a particular gesture, move in a certain way
- ask them to speak in a particular way
- discuss with them both how they might move or speak and why - for example to communicate a certain set of thoughts and feelings.

6 The short sequence can be repeated a number of times, until the directors have used up all their ideas about their interpretation.

Shakespeare's language

It is easy to look at the text of this play and say to yourself, 'I'm never going to understand that!' But it is important not to be put off. Remember that there are two reasons why Shakespeare's language may seem strange at first:
1 He was writing four hundred years ago and the English language has changed over the centuries.
2 He wrote mainly in verse. As a result he sometimes changed the order of words to make them fit the verse form, and he used a large number of 'tricks of the trade': figures of speech and other verse techniques.
On page 202 you will find advice on tackling the 'difficult bits'.

Language change

This can cause three main kinds of problem:

Grammar

Since the end of the 16th century, there have been some changes in English grammar. Some examples:
1 Thee, thou, thy, and the verb forms that go with them:
Thou canst compel no more than she entreat.
Thy threats have no more strength than her weak prayers.
Helen, I love thee. By my life I do.
2 Words contract (shorten) in different ways. For example:
'tis rather than it's
who is't for who is it
3 Some of the 'little words' are different. For example:
an for if.

Words that have changed their meaning

Sometimes you will come across words that you think you know, but discover that they don't mean what you expect them to mean. For example:

rude (Act 2 scene 1 line 152) meant *rough*. Now it means *not polite*.

weeds (Act 2 scene 2 line 77) meant *clothes*. Now you find them growing in the garden.

Words that have gone out of use

These are the most obvious and most frequent causes of difficulty. Shakespeare had - and used - a huge vocabulary. He loved using words, and pushing them to their limits. So you will come across many words you have not met before. They are usually explained in the notes. But before rushing to look up every single word, remember the advice on page 202.

The language of the play

Much of *A Midsummer Night's Dream* is in blank verse, but some sections are in rhymed verse and parts are in prose.

Blank verse

The main part of the play is written in lines of ten syllables, with a repeated even pattern of weak and strong 'beats':

These **are** the **for**geries of **jea**lousy

(ti **tum** ti **tum** ti **tum** ti **tum** ti **tum**)

If Shakespeare had made every line exactly the same, the play would soon become very monotonous, so he varies the rhythm in a number of ways. Often he just changes the pattern of weak and strong slightly:

Therefore the **winds, pi**ping to **us** in **vain**

(**tum** ti ti **tum tum** ti ti **tum** ti **tum**)

He also writes so that sentences sometimes end at the end of a line, and at other times in the middle:

I am, my lord, as well derived as he,

As well possessed. My love is more than his,

My fortunes every way as fairly ranked -

If not with vantage - as Demetrius'.

So the verse of the play has a strong but varied rhythm. Most of the lines do not rhyme, so they are 'blank' - hence the term blank verse.

Rhymed verse

Sometimes Shakespeare uses a pattern of rhymed lines. It may be just two successive lines (a rhyming couplet):
Not for thy fairy kingdom! Fairies away
We shall chide downright, if I longer stay.

Rhyming couplets often round off a scene, but whole speeches or parts of speeches in the middle of scenes are also in rhyme. For example, after the first line Helena's passionate speech to Hermia (Act 1 scene 1 line 181) continues in verse:
Call you me fair? That 'fair' again unsay.
Demetrius loves your fair. O happy fair!
Your eyes are lodestars and your tongue's sweet air
More tuneable than lark to shepherd's ear
When wheat is green, when hawthorn buds appear.

After twelve lines the rhyming lines are given one to Hermia, the next to Helena, like a duet:
HERMIA: I frown upon him, yet he loves me still.
HELENA: O that your frowns would teach my smiles such skill!
HERMIA: I give him curses, yet he gives me love.
HELENA: O that my prayers could such affection move!

The rest of this scene continues in verse, with plans, memories and thoughts about love all being expressed. But because of the rhymes we get the feeling that all will end happily. This is not going to be a tragedy.

Songs and charms are an important part of the fairy world. Titania's fairies sing her to sleep and Oberon, squeezing the magic juice on Titania's eyes uses the tradition of the magic charm, full of insistent repetition in the beat and in the words:
What thou seest when thou dost wake
Do it for thy true love take
Love and languish for his sake

Prose

In some scenes, characters' speeches are not written in blank or rhymed verse, but in 'ordinary sentences' - prose. If you look at the play as a whole, you will see that prose is used for certain characters and situations. Look, for example, at these sections:

Act 5 scene 1 lines 298-350; Act 3 scene 1 lines1-70. Work out what you think those characters and situations are.

Working out the difficult bits

If you come across a section of the play that you find difficult to understand, try any or all of these approaches:

1 Read the whole section through and try to get an idea of the gist of it - roughly what it is about.
2 Try to pin down which particular sentences are causing the problem.
3 Work out the pattern of the whole sentence - look to see if Shakespeare has changed the ordinary word order to fit the verse.
4 Try reading the sentence aloud a few times.
5 Don't feel that you have to understand every word in the play - very few people do!
6 Don't feel that you've got to read every note and explanation in this book - use them when you really need them.

Themes

Although it is very easy to pick out the themes of *A Midsummer Night's Dream* - love and friendship, dreams and magic, comedy or tragedy, attitudes to women... it is much more difficult to disentangle the threads.

When you are asked to discuss the themes in a five-act play it can be difficult to know where to start. The next section is made up of 'signposts' to some of the themes, which will suggest ways of starting to work on them. Like signposts on the road they may not take you all the way, but they will show you some routes to take.

Signpost: Love and friendship

Act 1
- Everyone who speaks in this Act has an attitude to love.
- Some are about to be married; some want to marry and aren't allowed to; some just want to get their own way; some love but are not loved in return.
- How does this affect their behaviour?

Act 2
- Is it possible that Oberon and Titania are still in love, but at the present time not good friends? Look for evidence.
- How does Helena see love?
- How is the relationship between Hermia and Lysander developing - before the magic - and afterwards?

Act 3
- How does Titania show her love for Bottom?
- With the help of the story summary, sort out for yourself the swings of love and hate and friendship in scene 2, the central scene of the play.
- Look closely at the words the lovers and haters use.

Act 4

- Oberon has set out to punish Titania, so why do you think he suddenly calls Bottom 'this hateful fool'?
- Titania asks Oberon to explain things. How is he going to do so?
- How are Hippolyta and Theseus getting on together?
- Does Demetrius sound convincing?

Act 5

- How do you think the play 'Pyramus and Thisby' relates to what the lovers have been through?

Signpost: Dreams and Magic

- Apart from Bottom, it is only the characters who have problems who become involved in magic and dreams.
- All the magic happens in Acts 2, 3 and 4 - except for the fairies' final blessing.
- With the help of the summary, and with the text, go through these three Acts and make a list of the characters affected by magic, and when it is put on and taken off.
- At the very end of Act 2 there is a 'real' nightmare. What is the point of it?
- In all relationships it is sometimes necessary to 'sort things out'. How might it be helpful for the characters to do this while in a dream or under the influence of magic, instead of in 'real life'.
- At the end of the play Puck suggests that we may all have been dreaming. In what ways might this dream have done us good?

Signpost: Comedy and Tragedy

The usual simple definition of the terms 'comedy' and 'tragedy' where Shakespeare's plays are concerned is that comedies end happily and tragedies do not. In the tragedies however there are often comic scenes and in the comedies there are often moments where tragedy seems about to take over.

Act 1

- Where in this play is the first suggestion that it is expected to end happily?
- What effect does Egeus' complaint have on us? Do you think it would be more or less effective if it were shorter?
- Lysander and Hermia are casually left alone together. Do you think this would be allowed in a tragedy?
- Look at Lysander and Hermia's exchange of lines about the course of true love. Does it make you feel that something terrible is going to happen to them?
- Helena has a soliloquy in rhyme at the end of scene 1. Read it carefully and decide whether the use of rhyme makes the content seem more or less sad.
- Use this way of looking at the other Acts of the play. Look at the story-line; at exaggeration; at actions; at the language; at the use of rhyming and blank verse; at the feeling you get when Oberon, Puck and magic take a hand; at the atmosphere created by Bottom and his friends; at the fact that most of the action is set in the wood, at night, ringed around by fairies and by fairy songs.

Signpost: Attitudes to women

- How does Egeus think a daughter should behave?
- What is Theseus' attitude to the father/daughter relationship?
- What is the law of Athens on this relationship?
- How does Hermia regard a wife's relationship to her husband?
- What does Theseus' use of the word 'fellowship' say about his expectations for his own marriage?

These five questions all apply to Act 1. In the following three acts Hermia, and more particularly Helena, have most to say about this theme. Oberon's actions tell us some more and the workmen have their own views about how ladies of the court are likely to behave.

Love

Love is one of the important themes of *A Midsummer Night's Dream* but not all the characters have the same idea of what it means. Working on your own, try to match the two lists which follow.

Attitudes to love are affected by:

• age	• Oberon and Titania
• envy	• Hermia and Lysander
• youth	• Egeus
• war	• Helena
• a belief in reason	• Pyramus and Thisby
• parental authority	• Helena
• feeling rejected	• Lysander and Demetrius
• the need to win a dispute	• Theseus and Hippolyta
• a feud between parents	• Lysander
• magic	• Egeus

There may be more than one possible answer to some of these. As long as you can find a short quotation to fit the pairing you have made, you are bound to be right!

In groups of 4.

Choose to be either Lysander, Demetrius, Hermia or Helena. At the end of Act 1 each of these characters, unknown to the others, writes a letter to the problem page of a teenage magazine.

- Write your letter.
- Base it firmly on the facts and feelings shown in Act 1.
- Exchange your letter with another member of the group.
- Write the answer to the letter you have been given as the problem page 'aunt' or 'uncle'.

Dreams

When you are asleep your brain is set free from the thinking it has to do during the day, so it gets to work on the things that are bothering you. Sometimes you remember the dream, sometimes you don't. However you may well wake up feeling that the problem can be solved.

The main characters in *A Midsummer Night's Dream* have serious problems on their minds. They have vivid dreams and by morning everything is sorted out.

Working in a group of 3-5 try writing a dream.
● Invent a dream that you might have had.
● Remember that dreams often have a very strange cast of characters.
● These characters can do unlikely things - people can fly for instance.
● People and things can be in odd colours.

If you are short of ideas, try this:
● Agree on a topic.
● Take one sheet of file paper for the group.
● Write the first sentence of the dream at the top and fold it down.
● Pass it round the group in this way until the page is filled.
● Open it up and read it to the group.
● No one must see what anyone else has written until the end.

When you tell someone about a dream you've had, you are usually far more keen to tell it than they are to listen. Their eyes glaze over after the first sentence or two. Shakespeare has got over this problem by interesting us in the characters' problems in the 'real' world and then taking us into the 'dream' sequence and out again.

Try Shakespeare's method:-
1 Choose a problem that needs solving. Either invent your own or use one from a newspaper or magazine.
2 Start and end with the problem in the real world.
3 Make the middle section the dream sequence that helps to solve the problem.
4 Write it (or draw it) as a storyboard for a cartoon film or television advertisement.

Some dreams are more like nightmares. Titania's dream must have seemed like one of these when she looked back on it. Lysander and Demetrius (Act 3 scene 2 lines 396-430) and the workmen (Act 3 scene 1 lines 100-106) were also plagued by Puck and led about the wood. Word has got about that the wood is haunted.

Imagine you are either:

- Titania
- Lysander or
- one of the workmen

and describe your nightmare experience to a local radio reporter.

You can bring the chase up to date and set it anywhere you like - a house, a park, a multi-storey carpark or a school for instance.

It is easy to overlook that one of the people most affected by his dream is Bottom, the weaver. When he wakes up he calls it 'a most rare vision' and he wants a poem written about it. So his dream is more like an inspiration.

Again in a group of 3-5.

- Look at all the scenes in which Bottom appears (Act 1 scene 2; Act 3 scene 1; Act 4 scene 1 and scene 2; Act 5)
- Discuss what he says.
- Discuss the way he behaves.
- Is he just a nuisance?
- Do the others like him or not?
- Is he clever or stupid?
- What is he good at?

When you have a complete picture of the man, decide how his 'vision' might have changed his life if he were alive today. Would he have become:

- a writer
- a professional actor
- a member of a pop-group
- a stand-up comic

- a professor of creative writing
- or what?

When you have decided, write a short publicity blurb telling his audience what he is like.

Magic

We sometimes use the word 'magic' very loosely these days. In earlier times and today in other cultures, magic is still believed in as a force in people's lives. There are different qualities of magic in *A Midsummer Night's Dream* . There was the superstition that if you spoke kindly about Puck (he was also called Robin Goodfellow) he would treat you well. Look again at the fairy's conversation with Puck (Act 2 scene 1) and at the tricks Puck had a reputation for. They are much closer to our idea of what makes 'a good day' or 'a bad day' than to our idea of magic.

- Plan and write a short story based on one day during term time.
- Choose the kind of good and bad things that happened to you and your friends that Puck could have been responsible for.

The more 'serious' magic in the play was not done for fun but to intervene in people's lives, in Demetrius' case permanently, since his magic spell was never taken off.

- From this week's newspapers find and research a story where Oberon's brand of magic would be useful.
- It might be a planning enquiry or some government policy with which you disagree, or a conflict in a foreign country, or distribution of food aid, or an environmental question.
- Retell the story, as a newspaper item, with one or more important magic interventions.

Comedy or tragedy

In the section on Shakespeare's language, and in the 'signposts' section we have already noticed several features of the play which prevent us from feeling that the outcome is going to be as tragic as Hermia's predicament at the beginning of Act 1 suggests.

The play does of course end happily, but there is a 'play within the play' which does not. In spite of this tragic ending the 'interlude' of Pyramus and Thisby is comic.

- Take a close look at the characters of the workmen and their ideas about their play.
- In your opinion are they right to be worried about how the ladies will react?
- What first attracts Theseus to the idea of this particular entertainment?
- Can you unscramble Quince's prologue so that he says what he means to say? You can either do it by punctuating it correctly, or you can rewrite it (with correct punctuation) in modern English.
- List the elements which contribute to making the play funny, instead of tragic. Include language, acting style, visual effects.

Round-up

As a whole-class activity: 'Any Questions?'

- Choose a panel of four speakers and a chairperson.
- A possible panel might be: Egeus, Lysander's aunt, Theseus and Titania. They should be characters likely to have contrasting attitudes.
- While the panel tries to work out what questions they might be asked, the rest of the class, in pairs, writes down suitable questions for discussion, based on themes in the play. For example: 'Does the team think that death should be the penalty for disobedience to a father's wishes?'
- From these, the chairperson chooses questions for the team to discuss, with the rest of the class as audience. Each question is put to each member of the team in turn until they have had at least one chance to talk about it.
- All panel members must give their opinions in role.
- The job of the chair is to make sure that only one person speaks at a time.

Character activities

One of the most important things to do when studying a play is to get to know the characters really well. Keeping Character logs as you work through the play will give you plenty of raw material, but it is also important to gain a picture of each character as a whole. The activities in this section will help you do this.

Interpretation

Understanding the characters in a play is not very different from understanding the real people around you every day. There are people you like a lot and people you don't like very much; people you trust and people you don't; people you respect and so on. The difference between these people and the ones in a printed play text is that the ones on the page have to be interpreted before they come alive on the stage or screen. To do this the actor and the director - or you - have to look at what the character says and the way s/he says it. This is all you've got to go on.

If you start with a minor character - one who doesn't say or do too much - it is quicker to find the evidence you need. You will then find it easier to tackle the more complex characters.

Egeus

Begin by asking yourself questions about him:
1 When does he first appear?
2 How would you describe the way he puts his case to Theseus?
3 When you realise he is asking for the death of his daughter, what effect does it have on you?

Then:

1 From the following list choose the words you think best describe Egeus:
loving; bad-tempered; impatient; gentle; concerned; fair-minded; possessive; severe; kind; good-natured; responsible; happy; furious; scornful; unreasonable; cruel; vindictive; suspicious

2 Using your list of chosen words, find a short quotation for each of them from the speech, as evidence for your opinion.

Some of the characters change, for one reason or another, in the course of the play.

Look at Egeus' speech in Act 4 scene 1 lines 154 - 159 and decide, on the evidence, whether he is one of them.

Theseus and Hippolyta

We do not have as much chance to observe Theseus and Hippolyta as we do the lovers and the workmen. We can, though, find things out about characters in other ways. Find out all you can about Hippolyta's life before the play starts. Theseus tells us something about her, and so does Titania. Then add your observations of her when she is on stage.

From what you have discovered:

1 Do you think she will find it easy to settle down to married life in the ducal palace?

2 What is Theseus' attitude to her?

3 Why do you think she is the only woman to speak in Act 5?

4 What is her attitude to the workmen/actors?

When *A Midsummer Night's Dream* is staged the producer often casts the actor and actress who play Theseus and Hippolyta as Oberon and Titania also. Can you suggest reasons why this might be done?

Oberon and Puck

These two characters are responsible for much of the mischief in the play. They can also be said to bring great happiness. Imagine that Puck has been caught by some humans when his magic powers are not very strong. The humans decide to put him on trial for all the tricks he has played.

Decide on a list of tricks and a list of people he has played them on. You might want to include a traffic warden, a farmhand, a shopkeeper, a grandmother, Lysander, Hermia, Egeus, but there are lots of possibilities. These will be the people who want him punished.

Which characters in the play might be grateful to Puck?
What characters can you invent who might feel happy about what he has done for them?
Which group do you think Bottom might be in?

In groups or as a whole class activity prepare and present the trial.

Secret files

In any play, the writer presents us with key moments in the lives of the characters and leaves us to work out the rest for ourselves. It is interesting to ask questions about those parts of the characters' lives that the writer does not tell us about. For example: Why hasn't Hermia's mother been able to stop Egeus demanding the death penalty for her daughter? What was Demetrius like as a child?
1 Choose one of the main characters.
2 Make up a list of questions about that character that you would like answered.
3 Build up a complete 'secret file' about your chosen character. Start with their childhood and go on adding information up to the end of the play.
4 You can make up as much as you like, provided nothing contradicts the facts of the play and the behaviour of your character in it.

Quotables

When you are talking or writing about a character, it is important to be able to back up your ideas by referring to the play, 'This is true of this character, because in Act 1 scene 2 she says this, or does that.' You should have plenty of this information for the main characters in your Character logs. It is useful to keep some of this information in your head. A way of doing this is to search for 'the ideal quotation' for each character - the one line that absolutely sums up him or her. For example when Hermia tries to get at Helena, Helena says 'She was a vixen when she went to school'. Is this how you see Hermia?

1 For each of the main characters find at least two short quotations of this kind - they may be something the character says or something another character says about them.

2 Go through your list and choose the best one for each character.

3 Work in a group and try your quotations out on the others. Make a group list of the best quotation for each character.

Comparisons

Because Lysander and Demetrius are falling in and out of love with Hermia and Helena it is easy to assume that their characters are very similar. It would be useful to compare them with each other.

Similarities	Differences
in love	Demetrius has managed to impress
young	Egeus
quick-tempered	Lysander has not
scornful	
rich	

Now make a similar comparison for these characters:
- Hermia and Helena
- Oberon and Theseus.

Grouping the characters

The characters in this play are in four distinct groups which overlap at certain points. It is possible to make a chart to show these groupings at a glance.

Choose a different shape for each of the groups of characters and go through, scene by scene, showing how the sets of characters overlap.

If you prefer, you can choose a colour for each set of characters and place the colours side by side when two or more sets of characters appear together.

The beginning of this chart is done for you.

Act 1

Act 2

Key

□	Theseus, Hippolyta Egeus the court	◇	Lysander Demetrius Hermia Helena
⬭	Bottom Quince & friends	〰	Titania Oberon Puck fairies & elves

Magical influences

A Midsummer Night's Dream is different from most other plays in the way that the characters are presented, because much of what they say and do is under the influence of magic. It seems as though the extreme love that magic pushes them into feeling, makes them say things that polite behaviour would normally stop them saying. But this is what often happens in a quarrel anyway.

Write down very briefly the impression you have of each of the lovers up to the end of Act 2 scene 1. When you have done this look at the way they behave in Act 3.

1 What differences do you notice?
2 Which version of the person do you prefer?
3 Name any of the characters who seem to have stayed the same.
4 Choose any two characters and make a list of the really nasty things they say to each other in the quarrel.

Write down your impressions of Bottom in Act 1 scene 2 and in Act 3 scene 1.

1 How does the magic affect him when he is with Titania?
2 How do we know?
3 Does he seem any different after his experiences? (Act 4 scene 2)
4 Would you like to meet Bottom? Give your reasons.

Writing about the play

Much of the writing you have been asked to do on the 'Activities' pages of this book has been personal or imaginative: telling the reader about your own response to an aspect of the play, or imagining that you were one of the characters in it. There is another kind of writing you will be asked to do, and that is writing about the play in a more formal way, for example:

> 'The play could easily turn into a tragedy. How are we made to feel that it will end happily?'

At first this kind of writing may seem rather daunting. It can certainly be difficult to prepare for and organise. The notes on these two pages are designed to help.

The question

What you must remember - first, last and all the time - is that you have been asked a particular question. You have not been asked to 'write all you know about *A Midsummer Night's Dream*'. So at all stages of your work you must focus on the question. And there are two key questions you should ask yourself about it:

1 Am I sure that I understand what it means?
2 What is the best way to go about answering it?

Information and ideas

Before you can plan your writing in any detail, there are two things you need to do:

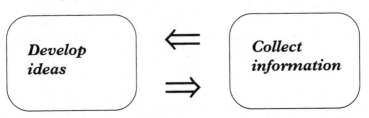

Develop ideas ⇐ ⇒ *Collect information*

Each of these helps the other. Build up ideas by:

- talking to other people
- jotting down lists
- making a web diagram

As you do so, you will begin to think of the information that you need. It is important to be able to back up each point you want to make by referring to something in the play - an action or a speech. You can use your Scene and Character logs to help here. As you look at the logs and at the play itself you will begin to develop new ideas.

Making a plan

Some people can write well without making a plan, but this kind of more formal writing is difficult to do well without any plan at all. This is one way of planning:

1 Make a list of the main points you want to make.
2 Think of the best order to arrange these in. Remember that someone is going to read what you write; you need to keep their interest, so don't, for example, use up all your good ideas at the beginning so that the second half of your writing is boring. Try to make sure that one point leads naturally to the next.
3 Your last paragraph should state clearly your answer to the question - which you should have proved by everything else you have written.
4 Your first paragraph should introduce the topic - but don't give the game away at the very beginning!

The right tone of voice

If you are used to writing in personal and imaginative ways, you may find it difficult to get the right tone of voice for this kind of writing. As with other writing, it is important to think about the kind of person you are writing for. If it is an exam or test question, then you may well be writing for

someone you have never met. So it may help you to
imagine that your reader is a teacher from another school,
someone who isn't used to your way of writing and who
doesn't know how you have been studying the play (and
who doesn't necessarily share your sense of humour!)

Writing topics

Sometimes you may be asked to write a short response to a
question or topic, while at other times you may be required to
write at greater length. The topics on these two pages give
practice in both.

Short answers

Each of these topics requires detailed attention to a particular
act, scene or part of a scene. The section referred to is stated
at the beginning of each one.

1 **Act 1 scene 1**
   In this scene Hermia is forced to make a choice between
   three unpleasant options. How does Shakespeare suggest
   to us in this scene that she is not going to be a tragic
   heroine?

2 **Act 1 scene 2**
   Compare and contrast the character and attitudes of
   Quince and Bottom using the information in this scene.

3 **Act 2 scene 1**
   What impressions do we gain from this scene of the world
   inhabited by Puck, Oberon and Titania? What powers do
   they have to affect the lives of humans?

4 **Act 2 scenes 1 and 2**
   What do we learn in this Act about the way women are
   seen and the way they see themselves in this society?

5 **Act 3 scene 1**

In Act 5 Philostrate tells us that this is the first time the workmen have put on a play. How would we have known this from watching their rehearsal?

6 **Act 3 scene 2**

The application of magic has unlocked behaviour which the lovers would usually be anxious to avoid. Read this scene carefully: which of the characters remain truest to what we know of them already?

7 **Act 4 scene 1**

'At first sight Oberon appears to be a wicked and sinister character, but he is not all bad.' Do you agree?

8 **Act 5**

In Act 5 Theseus seems to be saying 'It's the thought that counts'. What would *you* find enjoyable if you watched 'Pyramus and Thisby' as performed in Act 5?

Long answers

1 Write a careful character-study of Helena, looking for both her good and bad points. Do you consider that her character develops in the course of the play?

2 Discuss the various attitudes to love expressed in the play.

3 'Men have an unfair advantage in this world'. Discuss with reference to all the male characters in *A Midsummer Night's Dream*.

4 Puck has been described as a 'likeable villain'. Using what we are told about Puck and how we see him behave, consider whether this is a good description.

5 How does Shakespeare suggest that the workmen are not of the same social class as the other character groupings?

6 Find out all you can about friendship in the play. How important does it prove to be?

7 Discuss Shakespeare's use of the word 'dream' in the play.

8 'The course of true love never did run smooth'. What are the obstacles to true love for the four pairs of lovers and how are they resolved in each case?

Glossary

Alliteration: A figure of speech in which a number of words close to each other in a piece of writing begin with the same sound:
Making it momentany as a sound,
Swift as a shadow, short as any dream.
Alliteration helps to draw attention to these words. It is also over-used for comic effect in the workmen's play:
Cut thread and thrum
Quail, crush, conclude and quell.

Antithesis: A figure of speech in which the writer brings two opposite or contrasting ideas up against each other:
Hippolyta, I wooed thee with my sword
And won thy love doing thee injuries

Apostrophe: When a character suddenly speaks directly to someone or something, which may or may not be present:
She sees not Hermia. Hermia, sleep thou there
And never mayst thou come Lysander near.
....
And, all my powers, address your love and might
To honour Helena and to be her knight.

Blank verse: See page 200.

Dramatic irony: A situation in a play when the audience (and possibly some of the characters) know something that one or more of the characters don't. In a pantomime, for example, young children will often shout to tell the hero that a dreadful monster is creeping up behind him, unseen. In Act 2 scene 2 Lysander tells Helena:-
The will of man is by his reason swayed
And reason says you are the worthier maid
Lysander thinks his change of heart is based on reason. We know it's the result of having magic juice squeezed on his eyes. Dramatic irony can be used for comedy. Bottom's

friends run away when they see his ass's head. He doesn't
know, but says:

I see their knavery, this is to make an ass of me.

Exeunt: A Latin word meaning 'They go away', used for
the departure of characters from a scene.

Exit: A Latin word meaning 'He (or she) goes away', used
for the departure of one character from a scene.

Hyperbole: Deliberate exaggeration, for dramatic effect.
For example when Hermia wakes up and realises that
Lysander has gone, she jumps to the conclusion that
Demetrius must have killed him and says:

If thou hast slain Lysander in his sleep,
Being o'er shoes in blood, plunge in the deep
And kill me too.

Irony: When someone says one thing and means another.
When Helena thinks that both men are mocking her,
she congratulates them, but this shows she is hurt and
angry:

A trim exploit, a manly enterprise -
To conjure tears up in a poor maid's eyes
With your derision.

Metaphor: A figure of speech in which one person, or
thing, or idea is described as if it were another.
Demetrius, waking up after Puck has put juice on his
eyes, speaks to Helena:

To what my love, shall I compare thine eyne?
Crystal is muddy! O how ripe in show
Thy lips - those kissing cherries - tempting grow!

Oxymoron: A figure of speech in which the writer
combines two ideas that are opposites. This frequently
has a startling or unusual effect:

The dove pursues the griffin; the mild hind
Makes speed to catch the tiger - bootless speed,
When cowardice pursues, and valour flies.

Personification: Referring to a thing or an idea as if it
were a person:

O weary night! O long and tedious night,

Abate thy hours, shine comforts from the East,
That I may back to Athens by daylight

Play on words: see **Pun**

Pun: A figure of speech in which the writer uses a word
that has more than one meaning. Both meanings of the
word are used to make a joke. When Hermia and
Lysander lose their way in the wood and decide to
sleep, she won't let him lie too close to her. He protests
that he is telling the truth when he says his intentions
are innocent.

Then by your side no bed-room me deny,
For lying so, Hermia, I do not lie.

Simile: A comparison between two things which the writer
makes clear by using words such as 'like' or 'as'. Puck
describes the reactions of Bottom's friends when they
see his ass's head:

When they him spy -

As wild geese that the creeping fowler eye,
Or russet-pated choughs, many in sort,
Rising and cawing at the gun's report,
Sever themselves and madly sweep the sky -
So at his sight away his fellows fly

Soliloquy: When a character is alone on stage, or
separated from the other characters in some way and
speaks apparently to himself or herself. For example
Helena at the end of Act 1.